The Early Victorians 1832–1851

The Early Victorians

1832 – 1851

J. F. C. Harrison

PRAEGER PUBLISHERS
New York · Washington

BOOKS THAT MATTER

Published in the United States of America in 1971 by
Praeger Publishers, Inc., 111 Fourth Avenue, New York,
N.Y. 10003

© 1971 in London, England, by J. F. C. Harrison

Library of Congress Catalog Card Number: 78-137888

Printed in Great Britain

Contents

Contents

Illustrations

Work and Leisure

Social Propriety

The Visibility of Progress

THE AGE OF STEAM

CHANGING THE FACE OF THE LAND

THE CITY

SCIENCE

THE GREAT EXHIBITION, 1851

ACKNOWLEDGEMENTS

The author wishes to thank the following for permission to use material in the plates shown: the Science Museum, London (1, 2, 4, 9, 10, 63, 64, 65, 66); the Victoria and Albert Museum, London (36, 61); and the Wisbech and Fenland Museum (41).

General Editor's Preface

Social history is a comparatively new *genre*, though the name itself has long been familiar. It has been widely used as part of the combination 'social and economic history', as a label for the history of labour and popular movements and other topics of interest to scholars of the left, for miscellaneous studies of customs, social behaviour and everyday life, or even, as with the late G. M. Trevelyan, as a residual category of traditional history: 'history with the politics left out.' Its aim today is the ambitious one of writing the history of society. Ideally, it ought therefore to embrace and coordinate the numerous historical specialisms, since all are relevant to its task. In practice, social historians are, at least for the present, likely to concentrate on a number of topics which have tended to be neglected, or to be treated only peripherally, by the general and specialist historians, with some honourable exceptions.

Class and social structure is the most obvious of these, but the historical demographers have also opened up the study of the pattern of birth, marriage, death, household and kinship, 'urban studies' has explored the cities, while the pattern of culture (in the anthropologists' sense of the word) and ideas has attracted what the French call the historians of 'mentalities'. More generally, all aspects of the life and activities of the common people, that is to say those who have left little documentation behind as individuals, have been studied with increasing intensity. A great deal of work in social history has concentrated in these areas since 1950, when the subject began to be systematically developed. However, these studies have been unsystematic, both because the topics themselves have been treated patchily, and because other and equally relevant ones have been neglected. Though of course a good deal of important material has been accumulated by historians of one kind or another in other contexts.

The present series attempts to bring together, for the period from the industrial revolution on, what we know (and don't yet know) about the structure and changes in British society. Since social history is itself in the process of development, the individual authors have been left free to define their field, though they have all agreed to treat certain common questions and subjects. Though they are all experts, they have not written for a specialist public, but for students - of history, of sociology, or indeed of any subject which requires some understanding of British society since 1780 – and for the general reader, who, contrary to a widespread opinion, is not a myth. Not everyone who wants to know about the past and the present also wants to pass an examination. However, it may be hoped that the attempt to draw together the threads of our present knowledge, and at least some of those of historical discussion, may help to advance the work of the numerous and active force of social historians, if only by stimulating them to do better than the authors of this series.

E. J. Hobsbawm

Preface

The writing of this book was begun in September 1968 when the author was a visiting research fellow in the Research School of Social Sciences at the Australian National University, Canberra. My thanks are due to Professor John A. LaNauze and his colleagues in the Department of History for their very great kindness to me, and for providing the most perfect conditions for academic work.

The manuscript was read in part by Dr F. B. Smith, Senior Fellow in the Department of History, RSSS, Australian National University, and in whole by Dr E. J. Hobsbawm, Professor of History at Birkbeck College, University of London. To both of them I wish to express my thanks and appreciation.

In part of Chapter Five I have drawn upon material which I used previously in my book *Learning and Living, 1790–1960* (1961), and I am grateful to the publishers, Messrs Routledge and Kegan Paul Ltd, London, and the University of Toronto Press, Toronto, Canada, for permission to do this.

J. F. C. H.

Introduction

This book is intended to be a brief introduction to the history of British society between 1832 and 1851. It is not a sociological history, nor does it take a 'men and manners' approach. Rather it is an attempt to synthesise recent work in the field and indicate the way in which social historians in Britain and America are now interpreting the early Victorian period. The work of the pioneers in this area (J.L.and Barbara Hammond, G.D.H.Cole, J.H.Clapham, G.M.Young and others) is still indispensable for a study of early Victorian society. But this work was mostly rooted in the 1920s and 1930s, and in the thirty or forty years since then interest has shifted to new problems and new ways of sifting the evidence, though this re-evaluation has not yet proceeded very far. One of the purposes of this book is to convey a sense of the problems which face the social historian, to enable the reader to glimpse some of the difficulties as well as the intellectual excitement in recreating and analysing a past society. 'History,' said a very great social and economic historian, R.H. Tawney, in his inaugural lecture at the London School of Economics in 1932, 'is concerned with the study, not of a series of past events, but of the life of society, and with records of the past as a means to that end.' The historian's role 'is ultimately to widen the range of observation from the experience of a single generation or society to that of mankind'.

The period under review in this book begins with the passing of the Great Reform Bill in 1832 and ends with the Great Exhibition of 1851. Between these terminal dates lies a turbulent, confusing era variously labelled the Age of Reform, the Age of the Chartists, or the Hungry Forties. Massive events like the New Poor Law, Chartism, the repeal of the Corn Laws, and the Great

Irish Famine are played out amidst pedestrian political manoeuvrings and violent fluctuations of the economy. Statesmen, later to become the most famous of household names (Gladstone and Disraeli) hover in the wings; figures now long forgotten (like George Hudson the Railway King) dazzle the public eye for their brief period of glory. A young, attractive (if not beautiful) Queen is a refreshing change from the previous despised monarchs, her wicked uncles. Presiding over the nation in his unique role as a folk hero is the arch-conservative and victor of Waterloo, the ageing Duke of Wellington.

Some of these characters and events will appear from time to time, but they are incidental to the main subject of the book which is society as a whole. We shall be concerned with the total structure of society, the social relationships between groups and individuals, and the social institutions which define those relationships. The economic roots of these social patterns, the different life styles among various groups, and the corresponding ideologies will be brought out. Industrialism, urbanisation, improvement and self-help will provide dominant themes. In a final chapter on social mobility and social reform movements we shall consider problems of change, both sanctioned and rebellious. The regional and national diversity of Britain is seldom sufficiently emphasised by historians. Differences between town and countryside, metropolis and provinces, one main region and another, are mentioned in this book, but Irish, Scottish and Welsh readers may well feel that its bias is too exclusively English.

This last difficulty points up the limitations of a book such as this. Inevitably the writer of a general history has to draw upon the specialist work which has been done in various areas of the field. Sometimes these specialist studies will be plentiful and useful; at other times they may be completely lacking or only marginally useful. There are many questions which the historian would like to, but which he cannot answer, simply because he lacks the relevant data or monographs. It is therefore important to establish at the beginning what we know, what we don't know, and what we need to know about the social history of the early Victorian period.

Apart from politics, we probably know most about the economic background and the social costs of the process of intensive industrialism. A lively debate as to whether the standard of living of the working classes improved or deteriorated still continues, and has stimulated research into little-known aspects of the day-to-day life of labouring people. Because of the interest which labour and socialist historians from Karl Marx onwards have always shown in this period, we know a good deal about the various radical and social reform movements of the 1830s and 1840s. Examinations of the concept of class and the dynamics of popular protest have further deepened our understanding in this area. Recently there have been studies of the New Poor Law; and the shadowy underworld of crime, prostitution and pornography has begun to be seriously probed. The landed interest has been systematically described and analysed; and the respectable, self-help classes have begun to attract more sympathetic study than they once did. Literary evidence (novels, poems, and articles) has been well used to characterise Victorianism, and to explore, among other things, the social attitudes of the age. In general, the substance of this book has been drawn from those parts of early Victorian social history about which we know most.

But in writing it the author has been greatly aware of what we don't know, and where further research is necessary. Although excellent monographic work on Irish, Scottish and Welsh history has been and is being done, we have not yet reached the stage when it can easily be integrated into a general history of the British Isles. Ireland, except when events impinge on English politics, is seldom mentioned, and then always as a 'problem'. Scotland, with its very different systems of law, education and poor relief, is usually ignored; while Wales is simply lumped with England as a single statistical unit. This is to say that the Celtic fringe is virtually left out of the standard British histories, which are written from an English (if not metropolitan) perspective. For political history this is misleading enough, but for social history it is much worse. Most of the generalisations made, for instance, about social structure and social movements, probably need qualification in the light of the Irish and Scottish experiences. And the difficulty cannot be overcome by throwing in the odd example or illustration from Dublin or Aberdeen. Only a series of comparative social studies, concentrating on fairly narrow periods or topics, is likely to uncover significant points of similarity or uniqueness.

There are other, if less dramatically obvious, areas of darkness. Despite the excellent work of modern historical demographers, we still do not understand very clearly the relation between population increase and economic growth – a vital concern of early Victorian Britain. There is no history of the basic social institution in Britain, the family, nor any evidence of much interest in it among historians. The social content of Victorian religion has been largely neglected, except for occasional forays by interested parties. How long have we to wait for a modern history of Methodism, which will do justice to the social complexities of the schisms and connectional strife which plagued the chapels in the nineteenth century? Similarly for education there is a need to get beyond institutional histories, and examine the (largely unstated) social goals of educational movements and efforts. Working class culture, which has received some attention for its more recent periods, remains virtually *terra incognita* for the first half of the nineteenth century; although oral folk tradition, dialect, popular poetry and songs, and material on feasts, festivals and the use of leisure could be used to explore it. We also need more local studies of towns, counties and regions, to document the diversity and richness of our social heritage, and to correct the naivity of much 'national' history. A comparative approach is particularly valuable here, as it is also in intellectual history, which has been much slower to develop in Britain than in the USA. The social roots of ideas, including the ideas of the majority of ordinary people, have to be investigated before we can understand many aspects of a society. But such investigations have not yet gone very far into the period 1832–51.

This recital of the limitations of our present knowledge is not to be taken as meaning that nothing worthwhile can be written about early Victorian society, but that a healthy scepticism towards some of our accepted interpretations is in order. A final caution may also not be out of place. The early Victorian period has an air of familiarity about it, mainly because of our reading of the great novelists, especially Charles Dickens. Yet this can be very deceptive, for we no longer share many of the basic assumptions of that society, and our sympathies and responses are likely to be different from those of contemporary readers. They believed in immutable economic laws, in Malthusian fears of overpopulation, and in objective factors controlling man and society; we for the most part do not. Nobody in Britain today is prepared to accept poverty and gross inequality as part of a God-given order of the universe; in the 1830s and 1840s the affluent classes and most of the labouring poor took it for granted that rich and poor (like good and bad) would always exist. The barrier to historical understanding is not ignorance of the material facts of our great great grandparents' life (for we can easily look at pictures of them at work and play), but lack of sympathy for their fundamental ideas and attitudes. The world of Charles Dickens is a long way, mentally and materially, from us; and the distance increases every year. But if we can manage to overcome the obstacles to historical understanding we shall begin to deepen our awareness of our own society by extending the range of our experience through contact with the past.

The Social Experience of Industrialism

Population: or the fears of the Reverend Mr Malthus

It is appropriate that a social history should begin with demography. There is a rough logic in considering first the details of population, for in a fundamental sense they determine all else. History is about people, both as individuals and in relation to each other, and the number of people in a country at a given time is one of the crucial factors in determining what sort of lives they are likely to be living. Leaving aside other variables, a Britain of two and a half million people (as in the Middle Ages) will be a vastly different society from modern Britain with fifty-five millions, by sheer virtue of the difference in numbers; for the quantitative difference means also a difference in quality, and sets the bounds for the potentialities and limits of human achievement. We need therefore to establish in the first place how many people there were in early Victorian Britain, particularly in relation to earlier and later periods. Second, the geographical, occupational and age distribution of the population will give us important clues as to what sort of society we are dealing with. Third, movements of population will alert us to possible social changes that were in process. And lastly the trend of population – whether it was increasing or declining – will provide an overall setting for the period we are considering.

The most important thing about the population of early Victorian Britain was that it was larger than ever before, and moreover was increasing rapidly still further. The census of 1831 counted 24·1 million people in the British Isles; by 1841 the total was 26·7 millions; and in 1851, despite massive emigration from

Ireland, the figure had reached 27·3 millions.[1] This was a very high rate of decennial increase, though less than the peak decade 1811–21. It was of course a continuation of the trend which had begun in the later years of the eighteenth century, when after centuries of slow growth the population suddenly began to increase at an accelerating rate. The results of the first census, taken in 1801, had been greeted with incredulity in some quarters, as many Englishmen just could not believe that the population of England, Scotland and Wales was as large as 10·6 millions, with another 5·2 millions in Ireland. William Cobbett, the radical spokesman for rural England, denied that population was increasing: large village churches, he argued, were half empty on Sundays, which showed that the population must have been larger in past times, for our ancestors were not such fools as to build churches too big for their needs.[2] But by 1831 there was no longer any room for doubt; the fact of population growth was literally pressing hard on every side.

To account for this growth a number of factors affecting the birth and death rates have to be considered, though historians are by no means unanimous in their interpretations of the problem. In broad terms the increase of population from the eighteenth century onward was due to a fall in the death rate simultaneously with the maintenance of a high birth rate. But when studied decade by decade the matter becomes more complex. The death rate in England and Wales during the 1830s and 1840s was around 21–22 per thousand – compared with over 25 per thousand at the end of the eighteenth century and the early years of the nineteenth. At one time it was usual to account for this fall in the death rate by the development of preventive medicine, which reduced the risks of death from smallpox, child birth, scurvy and various types of fever; but recent researches have tended to discount the effects of the medical revolution. Although the spread of new medical techniques and the awakening of concern for public health provision ultimately helped to bring down the death rate, it is difficult to show precise effects in early Victorian England. In the area of greatest potential improvement, infant mortality, there had been a marked fall. Nevertheless the annual reports of the Registrar General for England and Wales showed that between 1839 and 1851, the annual number of deaths of infants under one year was usually between 150 and 160 per 1,000 live births. In the later forties the death rate for infants, as for the whole population, rose appreciably. All of which meant that the ordinary Victorian family was intimately acquainted with death in a way which is rare today. To ensure two surviving children a married couple could expect to have five or six births. The infant deathbed scenes so beloved by the religious tract writers, and the grief for the loss of a favourite child so often mentioned in contemporary biographies and novels were the results of these cold figures of mortality.

The corresponding figures of annual birth rates held steady at between 32 and 33 per 1,000 of population during the 1840s. Although when compared with today's figure of 17·5 this appears high, it was somewhat lower than in the preceding decades and also lower than in the mid-Victorian period. Unlike death, it was assumed that individuals had some degree of control over birth rates, mainly through the regulation of marriage. Since restriction of births through contraception was little known or practised, the number of births would be regulated by the number of years during which the wife was capable of child bearing, which in turn would be lengthened or shortened according to the age of the woman on marriage. If for any reason, such as hard times, it was argued, marriages were in many cases to be delayed, it would result shortly afterwards in a decline in births. Perhaps some such explanation lies at the back of the marriage rate fluctuations in early Victorian England and Wales. Until 1843 the annual marriage rate was slightly over 15 per 1,000 of population; but thereafter it rose to over 17, despite temporary checks in 1847–8. It is tempting to correlate birth and marriage rates with economic factors (such as the prolonged depression from 1837 to 1842) or with social policy (such as the tightening of relief through the New Poor Law of 1834), but the results are at best somewhat inconclusive. On the other hand, it is hard to deny some relationship with the almost traumatic experiences of economic depression and social misery which characterised the period.

How else are we to interpret the fact that in 1851 almost 40 per cent of all women in England and Wales between twenty and forty-four were unmarried; and that a total of nearly 2½ million persons of both sexes in this age group were single?

The census figures can be made to yield other clues of social significance. Take for instance the division of the population according to age. In 1841, 45 per cent of the population of England and Wales was under the age of twenty, and less than 7 per cent was aged sixty and over. Compared with the Britain of today this seems a very young society (the corresponding figures for 1958 were 29 per cent and 17 per cent), but it is not significantly different from such evidence as is available for comparative age groups in the seventeenth century. This would suggest that the age structure of early Victorian society was closer to that of pre-industrial Britain than to the pattern with which we are now familiar. Despite the great growth in total population, the traditional proportions of children, workers and old people remained about the same; though they had increasingly to adapt themselves to changed circumstances of life.

Some further hints on the persistence of traditional aspects of society side by side with great innovations are given by the figures of population distribution. From time immemorial the typical Englishman had been a countryman, and the census of 1831 showed that 961,000 families (which was 28 per cent of the total) in Great Britain were employed in agriculture. To these may be added the numerous country craftsmen and shopkeepers of the villages and small market towns, making a total of perhaps 50 per cent of the population who lived in rural conditions. The urban figures for 1831 showed about 25 per cent of the population of England and Wales living in towns of 20,000 people and above. Greater London contained 1,900,000 people in 1831 (13·5 per cent of the population of England and Wales) and by 1851 this figure had grown to 2,600,000. Twenty years is but a short time in which to chart population changes, but the trend towards urbanisation was unmistakable. The census of 1851 showed that for the first time in history just over half the population of England and Wales was living in urban areas. The path to the present day, when over 80 per cent of Britishers are urbanised, was already established.

Growth of population in urban areas was the result of two factors: natural increase (that is, surplus of births over deaths) of the local populace, and immigration from outside. The rate of natural increase in the towns was not significantly different from the rate in the countryside, but in both cases it was high. Employment opportunities, however, were better in urban than in agricultural areas, thanks to the development of industrialism and the factory system. Consequently there was movement to the towns from the villages and farm lands, which declined (at first relatively, but later absolutely) in population. The townward drift took the form of short distance movement in the first instance: migrants into the industrial towns of Lancashire and Yorkshire came from the surrounding rural counties. Small towns sometimes served as concentration points for later movement to bigger towns; so that the pattern of population migration resembled a series of concentric circles, with the large town in the centre. Movement to towns was particularly marked in the 1840s, when large numbers of immigrant Irish swelled the numbers of native English and Scots who were migrating to urban areas.

The Irish population statistics bring to our attention one of the greatest tragedies of the nineteenth century. In 1841 the population of Ireland was 8·2 millions; by 1851 it had decreased to 6·5 millions, and thereafter it continued to decline steadily throughout the nineteenth century. Supported almost entirely by potatoes, the Irish population had increased rapidly along with the rest of the British Isles. When the potato crop failed in successive years after 1845 Ireland suffered a famine, and a mass evacuation began. It has been estimated that about 700,000 people died and nearly one million emigrated (mainly to America) in the six years before 1851. In the peak year of emigration, 1851, a quarter of a million people left Ireland. The social and economic, not to mention the political, impact of such movement was very far-reaching. Yet the simple statistics of overall population alone tell us something important about Ireland in the early Victorian era. Today the Irish Republic and Northern Ireland together have

only about 4·5 million people, or 8 per cent of the total population of the British Isles. In 1841 the Irish population was over 30
per cent of the total, being half as big as that of England and
Wales, and more than three times that of Scotland. Proportion-
ately to population, Ireland was much more important in the early
Victorian scene than it is today – a consideration which is seldom
reflected in histories of the period.

To some of the implications of these statistics of population we
shall return in succeeding chapters. For the time being enough
has been said to vindicate the concern of the early Victorians with
population problems. Every age has its peculiar way of looking at
social issues, and Victorian Britain was no exception. It was in
fact firmly in the grip of Malthusianism which, in association with
the doctrines of political economy and philosophic radicalism,
proved to be one of the most compelling theories of the modern
world. The Reverend Thomas Malthus had published *An Essay
on the Principle of Population* in 1798, to express his doubts about
current ideas on the perfectability of man and schemes for the
improvement of society. Before his death in 1834, six editions
of his work had been published, and he had elaborated further
upon his 'principle of population' (taken as a law of nature) and
applied it to immediate social problems. The starting point of his
theory was the capacity (and constant tendency) of population to
grow faster than the means of subsistence. In practice population
was prevented from outstripping the means of feeding it by the
operation of vice, misery and moral restraint. These checks to
population Malthus divided into two categories: positive and
preventive. Positive checks included all causes of mortality outside
the control of the individual, arising from what he called vice
and misery. Under this head, he argued:

may be enumerated all unwholesome occupations, severe labour and
exposure to the seasons, extreme poverty, bad nursing of children,
large towns, excesses of all kinds, the whole train of common diseases
and epidemics, wars, plague, and famine.[3]

By preventive checks Malthus meant limitation of births by
means which are under the control of the individual, and which

relate to conscious and voluntary decisions. Some types of 'vice', such as sexual perversity and artificial contraception within marriage, he included in this category. But the preventive check with which he was most concerned was moral restraint. This he defined as postponement of marriage until a man could afford to support a family, together with strict continence before marriage. Since mankind could not escape from the workings of the 'principle of population', the only way to avoid the evil and unhappiness caused by the positive checks was to embrace the alternative of moral restraint. In so doing a man would rise to his full stature as a rational being.

Malthus was not the first nor the only writer on population problems in the later eighteenth and early nineteenth centuries, but his brilliant *Essay* appeared at precisely the moment when those problems were beginning to cause consternation among thinking men. By simplifying the whole matter to a clash between numbers of population and means of subsistence he dramatically presented his contemporaries with the need to make a choice. Not all of them, even among the orthodox political economists, accepted Malthus' theory in its entirety, but the *Essay* made a deep impression and defined the terms in which the population debate was carried on until late in the nineteenth century. By the 1830s and 1840s this debate was in full swing, and moreover was given a very practical relevance by the decision to reform the Poor Laws. A convinced Malthusian, writing in 1845, could state baldly:

Population must if possible be prevented from increasing beyond the means of subsistence. This can only be done by restraining people from marrying until they can bear the expenses of a family. Whatever other remedies may be prescribed, therefore, restrictions upon the marriages of the poor are an indispensable part of the regimen to be observed.

Though he had to confess that 'it requires some courage, in these days, to exhibit such principles, the very essence of Malthusianism, in all their naked simplicity'.[4]

The Malthusian theory was at bottom a very gloomy view of

society. A note of pessimism is inescapable in nearly all Malthusian writing, for even Malthus himself, for all his encouragement of moral restraint, does not seem to have believed that mankind would in fact follow his advice. Perhaps this helps to account for Malthus' domination of the debate: he articulated the fears and pessimism of a great many people. Today these fears still have the power to haunt people. Without the advantage of hindsight the early Victorians can hardly be blamed for their concern (even panic) when they saw the quite unprecedented hordes of people everywhere arising round them. They could not know that industrial growth would ultimately dispel many of their fears – only to create new ones. Nor that democracy would provide a means to assimilate the labouring poor into the body politic. They correctly perceived that this new population would result in a new society, and that discussion of population problems was really about the whole future of society. The fears of the Reverend Mr Malthus were not just fears of numbers of people, but fear of radical social change, even of revolution. Historians have exercised considerable ingenuity in showing why Britain was unique in avoiding a violent revolution in the nineteenth century. But in the following pages we shall see that to the early Victorians it seemed a matter of touch and go.

The Progress of the Nation

In 1847 George Richardson Porter, a statistician at the Board of Trade, brought out a new edition of his *Progress of the Nation, in its various Social and Economical Relations, from the Beginning of the Nineteenth Century.* The book professed 'to mark the progress of this United Kingdom, in which all the elements of improvement are working with incessant and increasing energy'. To enquire into the circumstances which have made one's own country pre-eminent, he argued, would almost seem to be a duty; but especially is this so in the case of the present generation, 'by which have been made the greatest advances in civilisation that can be found recorded in the annals of mankind'. Although he allotted one of the eight sections to 'Moral Progress' (comprising chapters on crime, manners, education and postage), most of the book was devoted to economic and financial growth. Progress meant essentially material progress, based on 'well-authenticated facts', from which could be drawn conclusions 'supported by principles, the truth of which has in general been recognised'.

The figures which Porter produced certainly looked impressive. Not one of his innumerable tables, covering everything from emigration and manufactures to taxes and food, failed to show a substantial increase during the previous forty years. By 1847 Britain just had more of everything: more raw cotton imported, more tons of coal dug out, more miles of railway built – also more crime – than ever before. Even the increase in population was taken as evidence of prosperity, and the dark fears of the Malthusians dispelled by the growth in food production. The early Victorians were the last people to claim that worldly wealth was the sole end of man's existence. Nevertheless the material achievement was so dazzling that at times they were quite carried away and wrote of it in lyrical, even transcendental language. They admitted that of course there were other constituents of progress, but none was so conveniently measurable nor so dear to the heart of a generation which, like Mr Gradgrind, had a veritable passion for 'facts'. Porter (with all the enthusiasm and brashness of the pioneer generation of social statisticians) thought that because his facts were unconnected with 'party feelings' or 'fanciful theories', they had an objective validity which put them beyond any questioning. Despite this myopia, his compilation from parliamentary and other official records was a brilliant plundering and a massive testimony to the unprecedented growth of the economy. Porter had difficulty, because of insufficiency of data, in measuring the growth of total national wealth. But modern economists have calculated that the total gross national income of Great Britain rose from £340 millions in 1831 to £523·3 millions in 1851. There could hardly be much doubt, in this sense, about the Progress of the Nation.

The developments which Porter was outlining have usually been described by historians as the second phase of the Industrial Revolution. Beginning in the second half of the eighteenth century with a series of inventions in the textile industry, this revolution rapidly transformed the whole basis of British life. The world's first machine civilisation was born and the transition to the 'industry state' commenced. By 1832 the first stage had been completed, with the successful application of steampower to new machines in the textile mills, the expansion of production in the coal, iron and engineering industries, and the concentration of production in the North and Midlands. The 1830s and 1840s saw an intensification of the trend towards factory production and a ruthless exploitation of economic resources.

More recently these developments have been approached from a somewhat different angle. In place of the idea of the Industrial Revolution, as formulated by Arnold Toynbee in 1881, we now have an interpretation which reflects the modern economists' interest in economic growth. Five stages of economic growth in the life of industrial societies are identified by W.W.Rostow and vividly labelled in language appropriate to the space age.[5] According to this nomenclature Britain by the 1830s had long since completed her 'take-off' (1783–1802) and was more than half-way through her 'drive to maturity'. During the forty years or so of this stage (which would be completed by 1850) the economy made sustained, if fluctuating progress as it moved beyond the narrow range of industries (textiles, coal and iron) which had powered the original take-off. A high proportion of the national income went into investment (thus ensuring that production kept ahead of population increase) and full use was made of the most advanced technology of the day. As yet however the main thrust of the economy was in the basic industries sector and the shift to consumers' goods and services was still in the future.

Whether we talk of take-off or prefer the older and more familiar term, Industrial Revolution, there are two aspects of the economic history of early Victorian Britain which have briefly to be considered. First is the pattern of industrial development. Porter's statistics, supplemented by the census of 1851, make it clear that the largest industry was still agriculture. Over one and three quarter million people were directly engaged in it, and when harvests were reasonably good Britain was virtually self-supporting in food supplies. With only a small increase in the labour force, agricultural production during the 1830s and 1840s was almost able to keep pace with the expanding demands of the town population. In the non-agricultural sector of the economy the textile industry dominated the life of the nation, as it had done for the previous sixty years. The numbers employed in the main branches of the trade were large (probably about 1,100,000, excluding hosiery and lace), but even more important was the role of textiles, especially cotton, as a pace-setter for the whole of industry in matters of economic organisation, industrial relations and technological innovation. In conjunction with coal, iron and engineering, textiles provided the basis of British achievement. 'It is to the spinning-jenny and the steam-engine,' observed Porter, 'that we must look as having been the true moving powers of our fleets and armies, and the chief support also of a long-continued agricultural prosperity.' Mechanical engineering had by the 1840s developed most of the machine tools necessary for precision work: James Nasmyth's steam hammer could forge a huge casting or gently crack an egg in a wineglass, while Joseph Whitworth produced gauges which were accurate to a ten-thousandth of an inch. No such technical progress was observable in the coal industry, which increased output simply by sinking deeper shafts and employing more men. In 1836 the mines produced 30 million tons of coal, and ten years later this figure had increased to 44 millions. Closely geared to coal as a main consumer was the iron industry. Continuous innovation in the iron-making processes greatly improved efficiency, and total output rose spectacularly from about 700,000 tons per year in 1830 to 1 million tons in 1835 and 2 millions in 1847. The basic sector of the economy (sometimes called the Great Industry) comprising manufacturing and mining probably did not employ more than 1·7 million workers. This was less than a quarter of the occupied persons listed in 1851, and only a fraction of the total population. Yet it provided the motive force for 'the workshop of the world'.

The second aspect to be noted is the fluctuation of the economy. In the years following the Reform Bill of 1832 harvests were good and the price of wheat (always taken as an index of food prices) fell drastically. Investment in home industries was stimulated and there was a boom in railway construction after the success of the Liverpool and Manchester line (begun in 1826) became apparent. The prosperity, however, was shortlived: in 1836 the good harvests and the trade boom came to an end, and by 1837 the country was plunged into a prolonged depression lasting until 1842. These six years were the grimmest period in the history of the nineteenth century. Industry came to a standstill, unemployment reached hitherto unknown proportions, and with high food prices and inadequate relief the manufacturing population faced hunger and destitution. At no time did the whole system seem nearer to complete breakdown. Revival began in 1843 and continued into the 1850s, though broken by another recession in 1847–48. A second railway boom in the mid-forties contributed largely to the recovery (between 1843 and 1848 the length of line in the United Kingdom was extended from 2,000 to 5,000 miles), and by 1851 the Great Exhibition was able, with some plausibility, to suggest that the 'Hungry Forties' were no more than a temporary interruption in the rapid progress of the nation towards prosperity for all.

That economic developments are closely related to social institutions and actions should not perhaps require much emphasis. But in early Victorian Britain the relationship was unusually prominent. The very rapid rate of economic development meant that relatively few people were fully abreast of what was going on in the country, the more so as 'Progress' proceeded unevenly between different parts of the country and in different sections of the same industry. It is hard to escape the impression that very large numbers of people in the 1840s were completely bewildered by the environment in which they found themselves. They were required to make adjustments of a far reaching nature: moving to a strange new place, starting a new type of job, suddenly being unemployed. Their past experience had given them few of the social skills required to cope with such situations. Small wonder that the period overflowed with social tension and frustration. The period 1832–51 saw an unprecedentedly large number of people involved in a variety of movements of social protest, which ebbed and flowed according to (among other things) the cycle of booms and slumps. It is in fact possible to construct a rough social tension chart,[6] correlating periods of maximum radical protest with unemployment and the price of bread – though it would be unwise to draw simplistic conclusions from such data.

To say that contemporaries were bewildered by the events of the 1830s and 1840s is not to deny that they had definite views about things. They could not, as individuals, do much about the fluctuations of the economy, but they could and did express themselves about the 'social problem' or the 'condition-of-England-question'. In so doing they were trying to comprehend the nature of the changes which acceptance of an industrial way of life demanded. The fateful initial steps which led inevitably to the 'industry state' had been taken long ago, and there was now no turning back. The potentialities of the new economy of growth seemed enormous, but if they were to be realised there would have to be acceptance of fundamental changes in ways of life and habits of thought. The Industrial Revolution was at this stage essentially a social experience. At the time contemporaries made many different diagnoses of the problems, depending upon their stations in life and ideological positions. If we are to avoid 'the enormous condescension of posterity'[7] we have to take seriously what they were saying, even though sometimes we may think that they were mistaken. After all, they were there and we were not. They lived through this phase of the Industrial Revolution and they tried to express their experience in meaningful terms. The problems identified by Chartists and professors of political economy, by factory reformers and Whig mill owners provide the key to the social experience of industrialism.

From an economic point of view the prime characteristic of industrialism is economic growth. This is the main evidence on which Porter relied to establish the Progress of the Nation – but he was well aware that this was not the whole of the story. Associated with economic growth are certain forms of social organisation and also (as was very evident in the 1830s and 1840s) social disorganisation, without which the expansion cannot take

B

place. Industrialism therefore implies social change, and the context in which this change takes place is indicated by the 'problems' which the participants identify – over-population, poor laws, great cities, the factory system. There need not in principle be any necessary connection between an industrial revolution, urbanisation and a factory system. Great cities existed in ancient times long before industrialism or factories; and historians have shown that 'manufactories' predated the Industrial Revolution of the eighteenth century. In Britain the three have usually been regarded as inseparable, but this is an assumption which is not very helpful in exploring the nature of early Victorian society in the first instance. For purposes of analysis the process of urban growth and the development of a factory system can be considered as independent factors.[8]

The census of 1851, as we have seen, showed that for the first time slightly more than half the population was urban. The period of fastest growth had been the decade 1821–31, but the increase was not much less during the succeeding twenty years. Most of what are now the principal cities of modern Britain continued to grow rapidly between 1831 and 1851: Manchester from 182,000 to 303,000; Leeds 123,000 to 172,000; Birmingham 144,000 to 233,000; Glasgow 202,000 to 345,000. Bradford, the fastest growing town in this period of the Industrial Revolution, had 13,000 inhabitants in 1801, 26,000 in 1821, and 104,000 by 1851. At the beginning of the century London (with nearly a million) was the only city with more than 100,000 population; by 1851 there were nine. This massive growth had come from both natural increase and immigration, the proportion differing considerably from town to town. In 1851 a half or more of the adult inhabitants of Leeds, Sheffield and Norwich had been born in the town: in Manchester, Bradford and Glasgow just over a quarter were natives; and in Liverpool the proportion was even less.

The facts of demography provided a foundation for the Victorians' great debate about cities, but the debate focused on 'problems' rather than numbers. Harking back to a much older tradition of rural–urban dichotomy, in which country life was assumed to be the norm and cities an 'unnatural' development which required special explanation, conservative critics of the new towns concentrated their attention on what was wrong. Cobbett's denunciation of London as 'the great Wen' is a picturesque and well-known example of this view. Reformers of a different stamp also joined the chorus of disapproval; and even pro-urbanites like the Reverend Robert Vaughan, who saw cities as centres of civilisation, adopted a problems approach. Vaughan's book, *The Age of Great Cities; or modern society viewed in its relation to intelligence, morals and religion* (1843), was indicative of the interest in the subject from the 1840s. Preoccupation with the problems of cities, however, defined fairly rigidly the terms of the debate, and precluded any serious consideration of the process of urbanisation as such. It became almost fashionable in Victorian Britain for writers dealing with urban developments to adopt a sensational approach. Such accounts are valuable evidence of contemporary attitudes on a multitude of social situations which happened to develop in cities. They do not, as some later social historians apparently thought, tell us much about how and why the urbanisation of the population came about. As defenders of the cities in the 1840s, such as Edward Baines, editor of the *Leeds Mercury*, were quick to point out, many of the problems of the urban areas (sanitation, housing, education, religion) were equally prominent in the countryside. So that the problems as such cannot be used to define the nature of urbanisation. The growth of population and its concentration in cities of various sizes is the great social change to be noted here: the problems will be dealt with in succeeding chapters.

One of the more unfortunate impressions left by an older generation of historians and sociologists is that all large towns in the nineteenth century were more or less the same – that is, equally smoky, soulless and horrible to live in. The tendency to lump them all together, ignoring any modifying differences, was in part derived from contemporary caricatures like Dickens' Coketown and encouraged by references in the 1840s to 'Cottonopolis' and 'Worstedopolis'. This is very misleading. Quite apart from obvious regional differences in traditional culture and economic and social relationships, the impact of population increase was very uneven. Not all towns were in the position of a Bradford or a Liverpool. Virtually all towns did increase between 1831 and 1851, but in some instances the expansion was relatively modest. Cambridge, Chester, Exeter and Norwich were of this order. Too often our impressions of urban growth have been derived from an over-concentration on the northern textile towns, though even among them their problems were by no means identical. London, again, was *sui generis*. In 1851 it was still by far the largest British city, though its position relative to the rest of the population had changed. The contrast with all other cities remained:

London [wrote Friedrich Engels, the young business man and future collaborator of Karl Marx] is unique, because it is a city in which one can roam for hours without leaving the built-up area and without seeing the slightest sign of the approach of open country. This enormous agglomeration of population on a single spot has multiplied a hundred-fold the economic strength of the two and a half million inhabitants concentrated there.[9]

Here the process of urbanisation had begun earliest, had gone farthest, and was more easily distinguishable as such than in the northern towns of the classic Industrial Revolution.

Closely associated, indeed often taken as synonymous with industrialism and urban growth was the factory system. Objectively this was simply a system of concentrated large-scale production, using power machinery and large numbers of operatives, together with the correspondingly necessary social institutions. In the 1830s and 1840s the factory system was still mainly confined to the textile industries. The Factory Acts were designed to regulate working conditions in cotton and woollen mills, and the home of the factory system was assumed to be Lancashire, the West Riding of Yorkshire and parts of Scotland. To establish the unique characteristics of the factory system it was, and still is, customary to contrast it with the previous mode of production, the domestic system. This was small-scale, handicraft industry, organised through a middle man and carried on in the homes of the people, often in rural surroundings. In textiles, relics of this form of organisation of industry continued into the 1840s, side by side with the factory system. The handloom weaver remained as a sad reminder of an earlier and once-prosperous type of economy; and in times of distress the older hands could look back nostalgically to this alternative order.

The complexity, and often sheer incomprehensibility of the factory system baffled many Victorians. A writer in 1886 remarked that after a hundred years it was still not understood.[10] His father in 1842 had declared:

The Factory system is a modern creation; history throws no light on its nature, for it has scarcely begun to recognise its existence; the philosophy of the schools supplies very imperfect help for estimating its results, because an innovating power of such immense force could never have been anticipated.

He emphasised its complete newness, and added 'the manufacturing population is not new in its formation alone: it is new in its habits of thought and action, which have been formed by the circumstances of its condition.' Nevertheless, the factory system is 'what statesmen call *un fait accompli*; it exists, and must continue to exist; it is not practicable, even if it were desirable, to get rid of it; millions of human beings depend upon the Factories for their daily bread'.[11]

With the last point there could be little argument during years of prosperity. But when the factories failed to supply millions of human beings with their daily bread, as was the case in the depressions of 1837–42, suppressed doubts and latent criticisms came to the surface, and the factory system was condemned as the source of all social ills. William Dodd, 'a factory cripple', was one such critic. Describing a visit to Leeds in 1841 ('I drew near the town and ... the tall chimneys of the factories became ... visible through the dense clouds of smoke.'), he noted

the many marks by which a manufacturing town may always be known, viz., the wretched, stunted, decrepit, and, frequently, the mutilated appearance of the broken-down labourers, who are generally to be seen in the dirty, disagreeable streets; the swarms of meanly-clad women and children, and the dingy, smoky, wretched-looking dwellings of the poor.

The factory system was for him an unmitigated evil:

> We see, on the one hand, a few individuals who have accumulated
> great wealth by means of the factory system; and, on the other hand,
> hundreds of thousands of human beings huddled together in attics and
> cellars, or crawling over the earth as if they did not belong to it.[12]

By the 1840s the term factory system had ceased to be an objective description of a certain type of economic and social
organisation, and had become a slogan or a convenient label for
a complex of social attitudes and assumptions. This is not hard to
appreciate, for the changes demanded by the new order were
terrifyingly fundamental and aroused men's deepest responses.
The factory integrated men and machines in a way that had never
before been attempted. 'Whilst the engine runs, the people must
work – men, women and children are yoked together with iron
and steam. The animal machine ... is chained fast to the iron
machine, which knows no suffering and no weariness.'[13] Reactions
to this phenomenon varied according to a man's position in life
and his social and temperamental attitudes. To some the factory
system was the practical application of Adam Smith's principle
of the division of labour; others saw it as a system of gross
immorality in which sexual appetite and precociousness was
fostered by the overheated atmosphere of mills; working men
complained that too often it meant the introduction of machines
that put them out of work; and reformers denounced it as a
system of child slavery. The factory system was all of these things,
but was not bounded by any one of them. It was more than
simply an aggregate of individual factories; it was a new order,
a completely new way of life. The spread of power looms was
for Porter an important symbol of Progress. For thousands of
textile operatives factory life was their social experience of
industrialism.

2

Patterns of Poverty: Labouring People

The pyramid of English society in the eighteenth century had been made up of ranks and orders rather than classes. From the 1790s, beginning with the middle ranks, the language of class crept into general usage, and by the early Victorian age it was accepted as a useful method of dealing with some aspects of the social structure. Very soon, however, the idea of social class became entangled with political struggle and theories of social change. Radical reformers began to talk of class conflict, and the concept of class acquired an emotional connotation. Awareness of social class spread from 'the middling and industrious classes' of the 1790s to the working classes by the 1830s, and a new, subjective element of class consciousness made its appearance. The arguments of Chartists and Anti-Corn Law Leaguers were conducted along these lines, though other reformers, such as the Owenites or the millenarians, largely ignored the element of class consciousness. The new terminology of class did not immediately supersede the language of an older, pre-industrial society, but continued side by side, just as the handloom co-existed with the power-loom or the watermill with the steam factory. Early Victorian society cannot be completely characterised in terms of class (whether used as an objective description of observable social strata or subjectively to take account of class consciousness), because of the survival of pre-industrial types of labour and earlier attitudes towards it. In the 1830s and 1840s the problems associated with an accelerated rate of economic and social change encouraged the new way of thinking, but the switch to class terminology was not yet complete.

The progress of this change can be charted in the evolution of the labouring poor into the working class or proletariat. For several hundred years the great majority of ordinary people in Britain were known simply as 'the poor'. A poor man was one who had to work with his hands to support himself and his family. He was not by definition indigent, though he was always liable to fall into indigency for some reason, culpable or otherwise (in which case, if he had no means of livelihood, he became a pauper). The Poor Law of 1834, for instance, affected the whole working population; everyone, that is, who at some period in his or her life might be in need of assistance. This vast army of the people of England was called the labouring poor. It was not a class in any significant sense, for it included everyone except a tiny minority of gentry, industrialists, and commercial and professional men. In comparison with modern Britain, the whole of traditional and even Victorian society was economically poor: the average real income per head in 1855 was perhaps £20, compared with £78 in 1959. The share of the labouring poor was seldom more than a bare subsistence – a position which was defended by Arthur Young, the agriculturist, with the traditional argument that the lower orders 'must be kept poor, or they will never be industrious'.[1] The great challenge to this position came as a result of the Industrial Revolution, when for the first time a vast increase in economic wealth opened up the possibility of escape from the ceiling of poverty which had dogged all earlier societies. First the rising expectations of a rapidly expanding middle class and then the creation of an industrial working class began to dissolve the age-old concept of the labouring poor. Poverty was still the lot of the majority of early Victorians, but the patterns of poverty (and also of prosperity) were more complex and the range of diversity was greater than in earlier societies.

Before looking at the details of social stratification it is useful to bear in mind the general position of the labouring poor in relation to the rest of society. Statistically the situation in 1841 looked like this:[2]

Engaged in Trade and Manufacture	3,000,000
,, ,, Agriculture	1,500,000
,, ,, Mining, Quarrying and Transit	750,000
Total Employers and Employed	5,250,000
Domestic Servants	1,000,000
Independent Persons	500,000
Educated pursuits (including Professions and Fine Arts)	200,000
Government Officers (including Army, Navy, Civil Service, and Parish Officers)	200,000
Alms-people (including paupers, prisoners and lunatics)	200,000
	7,350,000
Residue of Population (including 3,500,000 wives and 7,500,000 children)	11,000,000
	18,350,000

Unfortunately the census tables do not distinguish between employers and employees; but if we deduct about one million and a quarter as the number of employers of all kinds, we are left with four millions as the size of the labouring classes in Great Britain. To these should be added their wives and children, and also the one million domestic servants, giving a very high percentage of the total population. The overwhelming size of the labouring population and the numerical tininess of all other sections of the community are important factors in explaining contemporary attitudes towards labour, as reflected for instance in social policy or the apprehensions of the more comfortably off. It does not need much imagination to appreciate why the middle classes in the 1840s often thought of themselves as an island, surrounded by vast seas of poverty. In their factories, in their homes, in the streets they were continually aware of (because so dependent on) the labouring poor. Truly they agreed that, in more senses than one, 'the poor have ye always with you'.

After its sheer numerical size, the most striking aspect of the labouring population was its separateness from other classes. Between manual and non-manual occupations a great gulf was fixed. The distinctive mark of the labouring man was that he worked with his hands. No matter how skilled he was, nor how high his earnings, his social status was determined by the kind of job he performed. The most lowly, ill-paid clerk in Dickens' England considered himself socially different from the most highly-paid, skilled artisan. The manual worker was further distinguished by his receipt of daily or (usually) weekly wages, and by a fairly high degree of insecurity in his job. Labouring people in many respects lived in a world of their own, remote from the experience of the literary, articulate middle classes. Increasingly segregated in working class districts of the cities, with a mortality rate twice that of middle class areas, eating different food, wearing different clothes, and observing different social *mores*, the labouring poor seemed to some observers to be almost a separate nation. It was the future Conservative prime minister, Benjamin Disraeli, who in 1845 in his novel *Sybil* wrote of the two nations, the rich and the poor. Adventurous social investigators had to rediscover working class England almost as a foreign land – in much the same spirit as General Booth of the Salvation Army wrote *In Darkest England and the Way Out* at the end of the century.

The third general characteristic of the labouring poor was the great diversity within the category as a whole. Social stratification was dependent upon a number of factors, of which earnings, regularity of employment, type of skill, trade or industry, training and education, and geographical location were all important. The crucial factor was earnings, which were a pretty accurate guide to the state of the other variables. Thus if an artisan earned 40s a week it was highly likely that he was also a skilled man with a steady job in an urban environment. Conversely if a man was earning 10s a week or less, it would be a safe guess that he was unskilled, subject to periodic unemployment and without much education. Within each stratum or occupational group enjoying the same income, other factors could produce considerable modifications. Old age was almost invariably accompanied by loss of earning power, resulting from bodily infirmity or decay of skills. Size of family determined for many labourers whether or not they were above or below the subsistence line. The rhythm of family life produced a poverty cycle which was inescapable for most lower paid workers. A child in a labourer's family grew up in poverty. Then as he and the other older children began to earn, the family income rose and a period of relative prosperity followed. As a young single man, and during the early months of married life while his wife was able to continue earning, he enjoyed a modest sufficiency; but when his children began to multiply and his wife could no longer earn, he fell again into the state of poverty he had known as a child. By middle age his children had become young adult wage-earners, the economic strain on the family was eased, and a period of comparative comfort could normally be expected. But with old age came a renewed time of hardship. No longer able to earn as formerly, dependent on the good graces of a son or daughter, the closing years of many an old person were darkened by fears of the workhouse, and, most shameful of all, a pauper funeral.

Most Victorian writers, when describing their society, divided it into the upper, middle and lower (or working) classes. They realised the rough and ready nature of this categorisation, and usually referred to the working classes or lower orders in the plural. Unfortunately the convenient threefold division stereotyped a view of British society which has persisted down to the present day, but which is more a statement of ideology than a useful description of social stratification. The three class model is inadequate for comprehending early Victorian society because, amongst things, it does not permit sufficient account to be taken of the very important group of 'middling' people who were distinct from both the more affluent middle class and the bulk of the working class; and because it obscures the great diversity within the working class. When Henry Mayhew carried out his great investigation of labouring people in London in 1849–51 (subsequently republished in 1861–2 and 1864 as *London Labour and the London Poor*) he had to employ quite other categories in order 'to enunciate for the first time the natural history, as it were, of the industry and idleness of Great Britain'. He found it 'no easy matter ... to classify the different kinds of labour scientifically', and his four volumes document the detailed and complex arrangements which he discovered among different sections of the working classes. Seeking, as a pioneer social scientist, for a general categorisation of what he called the social fabric he devised a four-fold classification: those who will work, those who cannot work, those who will not work, and those who need not work. The first three comprised the labouring poor. Mayhew's material was limited to the metropolis, and it has therefore to be supplemented by surveys and observations from the provinces, rural and industrial. From these various sources we can construct a typology of the labouring classes.

At the top of the hierarchy was the labour aristocracy. This was a small group of highly skilled artisans, earning 30s to 40s a week, with fair regularity of employment and superior working conditions. Many of them were handicraftsmen in traditional industries and had served a long apprenticeship. They inherited the pride and prestige of being masters of their craft or 'mystery'. In many trades there was a distinction between the 'society' and 'non-society' men, or between the 'honourable' and the 'dishonourable' sections. Among cabinet makers in London, for instance, a small group of six or seven hundred produced high quality work while the majority of four or five thousand supplied the mass market with cheaper goods. The former were all members of a trade society (or union) and their wages, work-methods and marketing arrangements were regulated by custom; the latter were less-skilled, unorganised and forced by competition to accept lower earnings. It was estimated that the 'society men' of every trade comprised about one-tenth of the whole. They were printing compositors, breeches-makers, jewellers, watchmakers, scientific instrument makers, some cutlery workers, hatters, iron-moulders, shipwrights, and carpenters. The new industries also contributed their quota of highly paid artisans: locomotive engineers, first class fine cotton spinners, calico printers and dyers. No hard and fast line can be drawn between the labour aristocracy and the lower middle class. The economic and social position of a small shopkeeper or independent master was very close to that of a skilled and experienced artisan – as witness the career of Francis Place, the radical tailor of Charing Cross who began his career as a leather-breeches maker, and whose shop became a meeting place for artisan and middle class reformers. In the metal working trades of Birmingham and the Black Country, and in the cutlery trades of Sheffield, little masters and skilled journeymen intermingled in a complex series of economic and social relationships, varying from craft to craft and between one sub-division of the trade and the next. Similarly at the lower level the labour aristocracy shaded off into ordinary skilled workers, whose wages would be in the range of 20 to 30s per week. Many building trades craftsmen, tailors, shoemakers, skilled engineers and lower grade spinners fell into this category. They were artisans and had the habits and attitudes of handicraftsmen, yet without the superior pay and security of the very first class men.

Below them came the great divide in working class life: the complete separation of the artisans from the labourers, of the skilled from the unskilled and semi-skilled:

> The transition from the artisan to the labourer [commented Mayhew] is curious in many respects. In passing from the skilled operative of the west-end to the unskilled workman of the eastern quarter of London, the moral and intellectual change is so great, that it seems as if we were in a new land, and among another race.[3]

Mayhew saw the difference mainly in terms of education and higher intelligence. He defined an artisan as an educated handicraftsman, in contrast to a labourer whose occupation needed no educational apprenticeship. And he noted great differences in the interests and life-styles of the two groups. The trade unions (which, until much later in the century, were virtually confined to skilled workers) fiercely maintained the privileged status of their members. It was quite unthinkable that a labourer should ever be allowed to do a craftsman's job, or that the 'mate' or 'helper' should earn more than a half or a third as much as the skilled man by whose side he worked. In Bradford the skilled woolcombers did not drink in the same pubs with more lowly members of the textile fraternity.

When we turn to the non-artisan section of 'those who will work', we are met with a bewildering range of jobs and conditions that cannot be defined entirely by stratification. Relative

degrees of skill are hard to estimate and do not necessarily corres-
pond with earnings: thus more skill is required for handloom
weaving than for navvying, yet the poor handloom weaver
earned much less than a railway navvy. Regional, occupational,
even ethical, variations were vertical factors modifying the general
pattern of stratification. Factory hands, for example, were really
characteristic only of the northern industrial counties; most of
Mayhew's street traders were not found outside the metropolis;
and Irish immigrants were concentrated in a relatively few
occupations and centres. We have therefore to bear in mind that
the following picture of the less fortunate sections of the labouring
poor is impressionistic, a series of more or less localised types,
rather than an overall description which is universally applicable.

Among semi- and unskilled workers the factory operatives
attracted a good deal of attention from contemporaries. They
represented for most observers the heart of the new industrial
civilisation, about whose benefits or iniquities there was so much
argument. As always, investigators tended to find what they were
looking for: the lot of the factory operative was presented both as
a state of continual misery and as a life of modest comfort and
respectability. Here are two contrasting examples. The first is a
rosy description of the homes of the operatives near Messrs
Ashworth's model cotton mill at Turton, near Bolton, Lancashire. It was written by William Cooke Taylor in 1842:

The situation [of Banktop, the operatives' village], though open and
airy, is not unsheltered; the cottages are built of stone, and contain
from four to six rooms each; back-premises with suitable conveniences
are attached to them all. . . . I visited the interior of nearly every cottage; I found all well, and very many respectably, furnished: there were
generally a mahogany table and chest of drawers. Daughters from most
of the houses, but wives, as far as I could learn, from none, worked in
the factory. Many of the women were not a little proud of their housewifery, and exhibited the Sunday wardrobes of their husbands, the
stock of neatly folded shirts, etc.; . . . I found that there were some processes connected with the cotton manufacture which the women were
permitted to execute in their own houses. 'The pay,' said one of the
women, 'is not much, but it helps to boil the pot.' . . . I was informed
by the operatives that permission to rent one of the cottages was

regarded as a privilege and favour, that it was in fact a reward reserved for honesty, industry and sobriety. . . . All were not merely contented with their situation, but proud of it. . . . It is not easy to fix upon a statistical test for measuring the intelligence of the adult operatives. I found clocks and small collections of books in all their dwellings; several had wheel-barometers. . . . I have more than once gone down in the evening to Turton Mills, to see the operatives coming from work. . . . The boys were as merry as crickets: there was not one of the girls who looked as if she would refuse an invitation to a dance.[4]

A very different impression is left by William Dodd's account of a young girl factory worker in Manchester in 1841. After the watchman has knocked on the window at 4.30 in the morning, the girl's mother:

rouses the unwilling girl to another day of toil. At length you hear her on the floor; the clock is striking five. Then, for the first time, the girl becomes conscious of the necessity for haste; and having slipped on her clothes, and (if she thinks there is time) washed herself, she takes a drink of cold coffee, which has been left standing in the fireplace, a mouthful of bread (if she can eat it), and having packed up her breakfast in her handkerchief, hastens to the factory. The bell rings as she leaves the threshold of her home. Five minutes more, and she is in the factory, stripped and ready for work. The clock strikes half-past five; the engine starts, and her day's work commences.

At half-past seven . . . the engine slacks its pace (seldom stopping) for a short time till the hands have cleaned the machinery and swallowed a little food. It then goes on again, and continues at full speed till twelve o'clock, when it stops for dinner. Previously to leaving the factory, and in her dinner-hour, she has her machines to clean. The distance of the factory is about five minutes' walk from her home. I noticed every day that she came in at half-past twelve, or within a minute or two, and once she was over the half hour; the first thing she did was to wash herself, then get her dinner (which she was seldom able to eat), and pack up her drinking for the afternoon. This done, it was time to be on her way to work again, where she remains, without one minute's relaxation, till seven o'clock; she then comes home, and throws herself into a chair exhausted. This [is] repeated six days in the week (save that on Saturdays she may get back a little earlier, say, an hour or two). . . . This young woman looks very pale and delicate, and has every appearance of an approaching decline. I was asked to guess her age; I said,

perhaps fifteen. . . . Her mother . . . told me she was going nineteen. . . .
She is a fair specimen of a great proportion of factory girls in
Manchester.[5]

Within the textile industry, where most of the factory operatives
were to be found, wages and working conditions were affected
by a number of factors. The particular branch of the industry
(cotton, wool, worsted, flax, silk), the constant replacement of
one machine or process by another, the relative use of women
and children instead of men, and the vagaries of unemployment,
all helped to determine the fortunes of any one group of operatives. In general, however, a male factory hand in Yorkshire or
Lancashire (employed, say, as a third grade spinner) could hope
to earn between 14s and 22s a week. If to this could be added
the earnings of his wife and children the weekly family income
would be raised to 30s or more, depending on the age and number
of the children. The women were employed as throstle spinners
(in cotton) and as power loom weavers, and their wages were
5s to 10s a week. Children were frequently used as piecers and
paid 2s 6d to 5s weekly. In Leeds in 1839 male cloth pressers
averaged 20s a week, clothdrawers 24s 6d, slubbers 24s and woolsorters 21s – which compared favourably with 16s for tailors and
14s for shoemakers.[6] The situation in one Leeds spinning mill
in the 1830s was summarised thus:[7]

Year	Men		Women and Girls		Children (under 14)		Hours per Week
	No. employed	Average weekly wage	No. employed	Average weekly wage	No. employed	Average weekly wage	
1831	139	19s 10d	385	5s 3d	250	3s 2¾	72
1836	144	21s 6d	442	5s 5½d	307	2s 10¾d	66
1840	135	21s 8d	478	5s 11½d	409	2s 5¾	66

It was a characteristic of the factory operatives, as of some other sections of the labouring poor, that the unit of earning was the family, not a single breadwinner. No aspect of the factory system aroused more controversy than this, and the employment of women and children became a focus for agitation and legislation in the 1830s and 1840s. Some of the wider implications of this will be examined later. In relation to social stratification it provided another distinction between the élite of skilled workers and the majority of working people.

As the textile mill operative was felt to be the representative type of worker in the machine age, so the handloom weaver was the representative figure from the past. The golden age of hand-loom weaving (still within the memory of the older weavers) had come to an end before the conclusion of the Napoleonic Wars, but the craft remained attractive despite a fall in earnings. It was an occupation which was pursued in the worker's own home surrounded (and also assisted) by his wife and family. He could, and did, work at his own pace and to suit his own convenience. If he wished to work hard for four days and loaf for three, he was at liberty to do so. He was free from the irksome discipline of the factory, and if most yardage weaving was monotonous he could always break off for a smoke or a drink when he felt inclined. Traditionally many of the weavers of the West Riding had also been farmers, and the substantial stone houses with their third storey loom shops stood as reminders of a prosperous past. Handloom weaving was popular because of its freedom and because it satisfied the old artisan craving for independence. Unfortunately it was also, at least in its plain and coarser departments, a skill which was easily acquired. Little capital was necessary: a loom and lodgings could be hired in Burnley and Colne for a shilling a week. There were no restrictive apprenticeship regulations, and much of the work could be done by women and children. An assistant commissioner who enquired into the state of the industry in 1838–9, reported that in Barnsley thirty Irishmen entered the town one morning and set up as handloom weavers, though they had never done any weaving before. From 1815 to the 1830s the hand weaver's earnings were reduced drastically, and he was forced to work longer and longer hours and accept more onerous conditions for the privilege of getting work. By 1838–9 in Manchester the total family earnings of weavers of coarse fabrics averaged only 8s a week, and similar figures were reported from Glasgow and Barnsley. Although there were important differences between cotton weavers in Lancashire, woollen and worsted weavers in Yorkshire, and silk weavers in London and Coventry, the trend was everywhere the same. Selected groups of weavers who did extra fine or specialised work were able to make up to 16s a week. But such earnings were a sad reward for a once-proud craft.

The 'distress' of the handloom weavers in the 1830s and 1840s received a good deal of publicity, though little constructive help. They were, after the agricultural workers and domestic servants, the largest occupational group in the country, numbering with their families over 800,000 persons. Their reduction in status from respectable artisans to workers on the edge of starvation represented an important cultural shift within a significantly large section of the labouring population. It is easy to write them off simply as unfortunate casualties of the Industrial Revolution, outmoded handworkers who were unable to compete with the machine. But this is by no means the whole story, and obscures the essential nature of the impact of industrialism on the labouring poor. Only in the 1830s in the cotton, and in the 1840s in the woollen, industries did power looms in the factories compete fully and directly with handlooms. Until that time the two existed side by side, with the handloom weaver reduced to being an auxiliary of the factory, but not yet driven out of existence by competition. His role was to take up the slack in busy times, and to bear the first brunt of a recession. He also acted as a check on the wages of power loom operators, most of whom were women. The plight of the weavers was a vivid illustration of how helpless a section of labouring men could be when caught between the relics of the domestic system and the full force of competitive industrial capitalism. In classical economic theory the handloom weaver should no doubt, under the stress of severe competition, have transferred his labour to some other sector of the economy. But in fact this did not happen. Weavers for the most part would not, and could not, find other employment. 'Too great attachment to the occupation is the bane of the trade,' commented Dr Mitchell, one of the Assistant Handloom Weavers' Commissioners, in the 1841 *Report*. Quite apart from their strong desire to cling to an occupation which enabled them to preserve something of their traditional way of life, their opportunities of alternative jobs were strictly limited. They were barred from entering, or apprenticing their children to skilled handicrafts by the trade societies; they were not required in the mills, where power loom weavers were usually women and girls; and they seldom had the physique or strength for an outdoor labouring job. Their occupation, protected neither by unions nor trade customs, was wide open to anyone who wished to take it up; and the supply of weavers was always in excess of the demand for their labour. At the same time, as earnings and conditions of work deteriorated, more people became weavers; for poor as the remuneration was, it was better than starvation, and for some sections of the labouring poor this was the choice in the 1830s.

Thus was the handloom weaver degraded. The story was told many times over by contemporary observers and fully documented in government enquiries. Engels' vignette, written in 1844, may well stand for many others:

Of all the workers who compete against machinery the most oppressed are the handloom weavers in the cotton industry. These workers receive the lowest wages and even when in full employment cannot earn more than 10s a week. One branch of hand weaving after another is challenged by the power-loom. Moreover handloom weaving is the refuge of workers who have lost their livelihood in other sections. The result is that there is always a surplus of handloom weavers, and they consider themselves fortunate if on the average they can earn between 6s and 7s a week for fourteen to eighteen hours a day spent behind the loom. . . . I have visited many of these weavers' workshops, which are usually in cellars, situated down obscure, foul courts and alleys. Frequently half a dozen of these handloom weavers – some of them married people – live together in a cottage which has one or two workrooms and one large common bedroom. They live almost entirely upon potatoes, supplemented perhaps with a little porridge. They seldom drink milk and they hardly ever eat meat. A large number of them are Irish or of Irish descent. These poor wretches are the first to be thrown out of work when there is a commercial crisis and last to be taken on again when trade improves.[8]

Other outworkers, such as the framework knitters in the hosiery industry, suffered similar though not identical experiences. In order to sharpen our focus and thereby penetrate a little deeper than is possible in generalised statements, it will be helpful to look in some detail at the nature of this one selected industry. Hosiery manufacture was localised almost entirely in Leicestershire, Nottinghamshire and south Derbyshire, and this Midlands trade provides a case history in which the condition of a section of the labouring poor, the outworkers, can be studied. By the 1830s the industry had developed various branches in addition to the old staple product, stockings. Shirts, cravats, braces, socks and gloves were all manufactured. Most of the worsted hosiery was made in Leicester, the cotton and silk in Nottingham and Derby. In Leicester there had also developed a cheap line of stocking manufacture, the cut-ups, or straight down hose. The traditional wrought (i.e. fully fashioned) hose was made mainly in the county. The basis of all this manufacture was the hand knitting frame, which was worked either in the stockinger's own home or in the small 'shop' belonging to a master stockinger. Steam power was not introduced into the industry until 1845, and the domestic basis of framework knitting remained until well into the 1850s. Like the handloom weavers, the knitters had suffered a steady fall in their earnings since 1815, until by 1838 they averaged only 7s for a full week's work.

From the early nineteenth century two factors had combined to undermine the independence of the stockinger – the system of frame letting and the growth of middlemen. Although in the eighteenth century some stockingers had owned their own frames, by the 1830s this independence had disappeared, and virtually all frames were hired. The owners of the frames were of three different types – hosiers (or manufacturers), middlemen (bagmen), and persons not connected with the trade who let the frames solely for the profits of their rents. Among the varieties of middlemen it was not always possible to categorise exactly. But in addition to the 'putter out' who simply gave out the yarn for the hosier and collected the hose when it had been made, there were two types of genuine contractor. The undertaker, or master stockinger, contracted with the larger hosiers to supply hose, and then put out the work to a number of framework knitters. Similar to, and often indistinguishable from this type was the bagman or bag hosier. He flourished particularly in certain country districts, and manufactured on his own account. It was from the twin institutions of frameletting and middlemen that most of the grievances of the framework knitters stemmed.

Frame rents were by no means the only grievance, but the struggle for their abolition became synonymous with and symbolical of the general struggle to improve the stockinger's lot. Traditionally the rent for a frame was ninepence per week, but with the introduction of the new wider frames the rent went up. A constant complaint of the stockingers was the uncertainty and variability of frame rents. A full week's rent was paid whether or not there was a full week's work, and it was paid whether the frame was in the stockinger's home or in the employer's shop. In the latter case an additional charge for standing room was also made, together with charges for light, fuel, and needles. Thus it was not uncommon in 1844 for 3s in charges to be deducted from weekly earnings of 10s; and there were cases where men who had had work for only two or three days in the week found that they had worked for nothing else than the frame rent.

But, as Thomas Cooper discovered:

... it was by a number of petty and vexatious grindings, in addition to the obnoxious 'frame rent,' that the poor framework knitter was worn down, till you might have known him by his peculiar air of misery and dejection, if you had met him a hundred miles from Leicester. He had to pay, not only 'frame rent', but so much per week for the 'standing' of the frame in the shop of the 'master', for the frames were grouped together in the shops, generally, though you would often find a single frame in a weaver's cottage. The man had also to pay threepence per dozen to the 'master' for 'giving out' of the work. He had also to pay so much per dozen to the female 'seamer' of the hose. And he had also oil to buy for his machine, and lights to pay for in the darker half of the year. All the deductions brought the average earnings of the stocking-weaver to four and sixpence per week. I found this to be a truth confirmed on every hand.

And when he was 'in work', the man was evermore experiencing some new attempt at grinding him down to a lower sum per dozen for the weaving, or at 'docking' him so much per dozen for alleged faults in his work; while sometimes – and even for several weeks together – he experienced the most grievous wrong of all. The 'master' not being able to obtain full employment for all the frames he rented of the manufacturer, but perhaps only half employ for them – distributed, or 'spread' the work over all the frames. . . . But the foul grievance was this: each man had to pay a whole week's frame rent, although he had only half a week's work! Thus while the poor miserable weaver knew that this half-week's work, after all the deductions, would produce him such a mere pittance that he could only secure a scant share of the meanest food, he remembered that the owner of the frame had the full rent per week, and the middlemen or 'master' had also his weekly pickings secured to him.

Again; a kind of hose would be demanded for which the frame needed a deal of troublesome and tedious altering. But the poor weaver was expected to make all the alterations himself. And sometimes he could not begin his week's weaving until a day, or a day and a half, had been spent in making the necessary alterations. Delay was also a custom on Monday mornings. The working man must call again. He was too early. And, finally, all the work was ended. The warehouses were glutted, and the hosiery firms had no orders. This came again and again, in Leicester and Loughborough and Hinckley, and the framework knitting villages of the county, until, when a little prosperity returned, no one expected it to continue.[9]

Cooper's final hint that the low condition of framework knitters was due to more than the specific grievances already listed sets the problem in a somewhat wider perspective. The distress of the stockingers, caused by their low earnings and long periods of complete or partial unemployment, was not the result of competition between the economically dying handworker and production by power machinery. The truth was that the trade of framework knitting, like that of handloom weaving, was overstocked with labour. Only in exceptionally prosperous times was there enough work to go round. The system of frame rents directly encouraged employers to spread the work over as many knitters as possible, even though this meant that each would have less than a full week's work, since thereby the maximum number of rents would be obtained. The organisation of the industry was well calculated to encourage over-crowding; there was, in fact, a premium on idleness. The industry was very susceptible to changes in fashion; new lines or new markets, offering higher rates than the average, attracted fresh workers, who remained to swell the numbers in the industry long after the temporary boom had gone. Entry into the trade was easy. Apprenticeship had decayed or become meaningless by the 1840s, and in any case the work was normally only semi-skilled. Youths and girls in their teens could easily manage an ordinary frame. The concentration of the industrial life of the area upon hosiery restricted alternative job opportunities, and it was customary for children to follow their fathers at the frame.

The two previous examples, stockingers and weavers, were of workers whose status and earnings had been drastically reduced. In part this had been possible because of the existence of more lowly members of the labouring poor, who in effect functioned as a reserve army of labour to depress wages. Beyond the ranks of artisans and operatives was an army of manual labourers, men whose bodily toil supplied the motive power for innumerable operations which today are done by machines. We are so accustomed to hearing about the great changes wrought by power driven machinery in certain industries that it is easy to forget how little mechanisation there was in great areas of early Victorian life. A vast amount of wheeling, dragging, hoisting, carrying, lifting, digging, tunnelling, draining, trenching, hedging, embanking, blasting, breaking, scouring, sawing, felling, reaping, mowing, picking, sifting, and threshing was done by sheer muscular effort, day in, day out. Much of this labour was arduous and uninteresting, and some of it was dangerous. It had to be performed out-of-doors with inadequate protection from the constant rain and raw cold of the British climate, or in the stifling heat and dust-laden atmosphere of the mines. It was not highly regarded: on the contrary, such labour was looked down on by all who could find alternative employment. No amount of moralising by middle class authors about the glory of work or the nobility of labour could disguise the reality. Rather was it the curse of Adam for a majority of the labouring poor. By modern Western standards labour was cheap, and it was used prodigally. Manual labouring jobs were so numerous and various that they defy any easy general description. We shall therefore, as in the case of the other sections of the labouring poor, have to confine ourselves to a few selected groups of workers.

The largest single category in any industry was the agricultural labourers. In 1851 they numbered over one million. There were also 364,000 indoor farm servants (of both sexes), making a total of nearly one and a half million wage workers in agriculture. They were employed by slightly more than half the total number of farmers, the remainder of the farms being too small to need hired labour. The number of labourers per farm and the type of job they performed varied between counties. In areas where there were many small holdings, as in south-eastern England, or in hilly areas like Wales and the Pennine counties, there were relatively fewer wage labourers than on the large farms of eastern England and south-eastern Scotland. Within the large county of Yorkshire several types of agricultural organisation existed, resulting in a difference in the proportion of labourers between one district and the next. The West Riding, although the home of the new manufactures, still contained some purely agricultural districts, and many more in which industrial and agicultural pursuits were combined. There was not only the seasonal migration of the woolcombers, for example, from Craven to work in the corn harvest in the plain of York, but also some continuation of the weaver-farmer tradition which Defoe had noted a hundred years earlier. James Caird, the agriculturist, described the small clothiers of the West Riding in 1851:

Besides those employed in the large mills, there is a class called 'clothiers', who hold a considerable portion of the land within several miles of the manufacturing towns; they have looms in their houses, and unite the business of weavers and farmers. When trade is good the farm is neglected; when trade is dull the weaver becomes a more attentive farmer. His holding is generally under twenty acres, and his chief stock consists of dairy cows, with a horse to convey his manufactured goods and his milk to market. This union of trades has been long in existence in this part of the country, but it seldom leads to much success on the part of the weaver-farmer himself, and the land he occupies is believed to be the worst managed in the district.[10]

Such men were of more substance and independence than agricultural wage labourers, as also were the small farmers of the Dales. But they did not hire help. On the southern and eastern sides of the West Riding were larger arable farms, on which wage labourers were employed, and on a model farm in this area Caird instances wages of 14s, 13s, and 12s a week for ploughmen, according to ability.

Something of the tradition of an independent peasantry probably survived into the mid-decades of the nineteenth century in parts of the North Riding. But the custom of annual hirings in Stokesley, Thirsk, Pickering, York, and the larger villages of the North Riding is alone sufficient evidence of the extent to which a large class of landless agricultural labourers existed in the district. In the East Riding this was even more so. There, in an area of rolling chalk wolds, the farms were large, anything from 300 to 1,300 acres, with large corn fields of 30 to 70 acres each; and 'the farmers are probably the wealthiest men of their class in the county'.[11] Mary Simpson, the daughter of the Vicar of Boynton and Carnaby with Fraisthorpe (an extensive parish on the eastern side of the Wolds), described such an agricultural district in a letter of July 1856:

This is a very scattered parish, entirely agricultural. I do not know if in any other part of England the population and customs are quite similar. Every farm (there are twelve in this parish) comprises in its household from six or seven to twenty plough lads, according to the size of the farms; their ages varying from about fourteen to twenty-four, but the greater part in their teens. These are all changed every year at Martinmas [i.e. the last week in November].[12]

In this, the most purely agricultural area of Yorkshire, a landless agricultural working class formed the bulk of the population. Living in the farm houses were the 'farm servants', usually lads and lasses in their teens. They were hired annually at the Martinmas hirings, and usually changed farms each year. During working hours they were supervised by a foreman and (the girls) by the mistress of the house. Board and lodging were provided, and wages – varying according to age – were seldom paid more frequently than two or three times a year. Upon marriage the farm servants moved out of the farm house, and set up home for themselves.

These two groups, the farm servants and regular outdoor agricultural labourers, formed the bulk of the farm labour force. Casual labour was also used: Irishmen, women and children, and textile workers (like the woolcombers mentioned earlier) would be brought in for the harvest. Among the regular labourers there was sometimes a degree of specialisation: shepherds, ploughmen, waggoners. But for the most part the agricultural labourer was expected to turn his hand to whatever the season of the year required. Wage rates were higher in the northern counties of England than in the South, varying from as much as 14s in the West Riding to 7s in Gloucestershire, Wiltshire and Suffolk. Unlike his urban counterpart, the agricultural labourer sometimes had additional benefits in kind. A tied cottage was often only a damp hovel; the proverbial pig and patch of garden might be but a poor relic of the once 'bold peasantry of England'; and it is impossible to know how many labourers enjoyed even these modest 'extras' and how many not. Where they did exist they perhaps helped to mitigate slightly the rigours of family life on 10s a week. Where they did not, recourse to poor relief was inevitable, as the swollen poor rates of the early 1830s attest.

For twenty years previously Cobbett had thundered against the degradation of the agricultural labourers to a race of potato-eating, tea-drinking serfs. His description of their condition was borne out by others. William Howitt, a popular author and journalist, who was anxious to take a favourable, even sentimental view of rural England, had to admit that the upbringing of the ordinary farm labourer made him little better than an animal. After describing how the labourer's children are set to perform small tasks from the earliest possible age, he continued:

They are mighty useful animals in their day and generation, and as they get bigger, they successively learn to drive plough, and then to hold it; to drive the team, and finally to do all the labours of a man. This is the growing up of a farm servant. All this time he is learning his business, but he is learning nothing else, – he is growing up into a tall, long, smock-frocked, straw-hatted, ankle-booted fellow, with a gait as graceful as one of his own plough-bullocks. He has grown up, and gone to service; and there he is, as simple, as ignorant, and as laborious a creature as one of the wagon-horses that he drives. The mechanic sees his weekly newspaper over his pipe and pot; but the clod-hopper, the chopstick, the hawbuck, the hind, the Johnny-raw, or by whatever name, in whatever district he may be called, is everywhere the same, - he sees no newspaper, and if he did, he could not read it; and if he hears his master reading it, ten to one but he drops asleep over it. In fact, he has no interest in it. .... He is as much of an animal as air and exercise, strong living and sound sleeping can make him, and he is nothing more.[13]

Allowing for Howitt's middle class, townsman's prejudices, this unflattering passage is a fair example of the educated early Victorian's view of the agricultural labourer. It was an attitude of pity and contempt, mixed sometimes with compassion and occasionally with fear.

Probably the most upsetting thing that could happen in an agricultural village in the 1830s and 1840s was the arrival of the railway. The decision to bring the line through a particular district had far-reaching economic and social consequences for that area. But the immediate impact was the arrival of a small army of construction workers to build the track. These were the navvies, a body of men who in the space of a few decades accomplished feats of construction which dwarfed the building of the pyramids in the ancient world (as the Victorians noted) or (moderns might add) the motorways of the present day. Strictly, the navvies were not common labourers. Originally they had worked on the canals (hence the name navigators, shortened to navvies), and they stayed together as a body, moving from one line to the next as it was completed. They were prepared to go anywhere that the railway contractors wanted them, later to France, South America, Canada, Australia and the Crimea. Not all of the 200,000 men working on new lines in 1845 were true navvies: some were agricultural labourers who were recruited locally, but it is probable that some of these remained to become regular navvies. The main attraction of the job was its relatively high pay. In a bad year such as 1843, weekly wages were 15s or 16s 6d; in 1846 (a good year) they were 22s 6d and 24s. These rates were for pickmen and shovellers. Skilled men such as masons and bricklayers could earn up to 21s in 1843 and 33s in 1846.

The work was extremely hard and often dangerous. A navvy was expected to shovel about twenty tons of earth and rock a day on the basic jobs of cutting, banking and tunnelling. Excavating was done with pick and shovel, the navvies working in rows. The men worked in gangs under the direction of a ganger who could be either a foreman paid by the sub-contractor or an independent agent who contracted the work from the sub-contractor. In either case the ganger recruited the navvies. Wet weather frequently created slippery, and therefore dangerous conditions. The earth from the bottom of a cutting, for instance, had to be taken out in barrows hauled up the steep sides of the cutting, and it was easy to slip and fall beneath the overturned barrow-load of 'muck'. Tunnels were nearly always deep in mud, and in addition there was the danger hazard of the crude methods of blasting. The casualties on the notorious Woodhead tunnel between Sheffield and Manchester (1839–45) read like battle figures: 32 killed, 140 seriously wounded, 400 lesser accidents. Edwin Chadwick, the Poor Law and sanitary reformer, calculated later that this was 3 per cent of the labour force killed and 14 per cent wounded. Compensation for injuries and death was seldom paid by the contractors or railway companies: a small payment from the navvies' own contributory sick club was all that was available. Because navvies were constantly moving on as the line advanced no settled mode of life was possible. They lived in rough shanty towns, hastily thrown together, miles from any village. Their huts were made of mud or wood, with tarpaulins for the roof. They slept in tiers of bunks, twenty or thirty to a room. No family or home life was possible; they might as well have been in Van Diemen's Land.

The reputation of the navvies was fearsome, and not without good cause. Superior physical strength, combined with barbarian bravado and high spirits marked them off from other labourers. They ate and drank more than any other men: two pounds of meat, two pounds of bread and five quarts of ale a day was normal navvy fare. Most of their earnings went in drink. After a pay-day (which the companies preferred to keep as infrequent as possible in order to strengthen their truck system) navvies would be drunk for days together, and there were plenty of stories of navvies (always known by their nicknames – Rainbow Peg, Gipsy Joe, Streaky Dick) who worked in a perpetual state of inebriation. Above all there were the fights and riots. Once the navvies had got the drink in them they were a terror to the surrounding countryside. Their drunken revelry (called a 'randy') ended in personal fighting and violence, and sometimes in riots between Irishmen and the rest. Few women lived in the camps; only old women to cook and wash, and some girls who were concubines. The popular image of the navvy as a violent, god-less, drunken fellow, far removed from the 'refining' influences of home and family, contained much truth. At the same time it also had to be admitted that the navvy was 'the king of labourers'.[14]

Another worker who performed the same type of sheer, hard muscular toil as the navvy was the coalminer. Traditionally he too was regarded as an uncouth savage, whose job and living habits segregated him from other sections of the labouring poor. Like the navvy he earned rather more than most labourers, but again his job was specialised and some aspects of it required skill. Wages varied between districts and between good and bad years, but a range of 15s to 25s was usual in the period 1830–50. For this the miner worked an 11 to 12 hour day for 4½ days a week. The work was hard and dangerous. At the coal face the hewers, naked and on their knees, hacked away at the coal with their picks. In narrow seams, which could be as low as 2ft 3ins in parts of the Yorkshire coalfields, the face worker had to lie on his side, use his elbow as a lever, and pick away at the coal. Behind him the 'hurriers' dragged away the cut coal in wheelless tubs or small trucks to the pit bottom, where it was hoisted to the surface or, in more primitive pits, carried up ladders in corves on the backs of women and boys. The transport of the coal underground, heavy and laborious as it was, was done by older children and women in some areas. Small children, as young as five to eight years, were employed as 'trappers', whose job was to open and close the doors as the tubs went by so that the air circulation would be maintained. The 1841 census showed 2,350 of the 118,000 coalminers in Great Britain as women, and these were mostly in the West Riding, Lancashire and Scottish pits. Some miners still worked by the flickering light of a candle, even after the perfection of the Davy safety lamp which, they complained, did not give enough light. The danger from an explosion of firedamp was great. For those who were spared this holocaust the daily accidents of broken limbs and lacerations, and the final inflammation of the lungs ('black spittle') left them scarred for life. In the coalfield areas it was easy to pick out a miner from among other people by his peculiar physical development and his habit of squatting on his heels. The coalminer was not normally a town worker, but lived in industrial villages in Northumberland and Durham, South Yorkshire or the Midlands. Mining communities tended to be self-contained and semi-rural, dependent on the single industry.

The urban labourers were much less homogeneous. They included dock workers of many different kinds; labourers in gasworks, brickyards, breweries, and ironworks; hodmen and helpers on building sites; carters, draymen, porters and sweepers. None of them enjoyed anything that could be called security of employment; they were paid by the week or the day. In 'good' times they could normally look forward to having a job for most of the year, subject to the important fluctuations of the weather and their own health and strength. But in times of depression, which were all too numerous in the 1830s and 1840s, the job outlook was bleak indeed: the weakest quickly went to the wall, and the strongest were reduced to the position of casual labour. In some occupations, such as work on the docks, labour was always hired by the day. The following account of the London coalheavers, based on Mayhew, gives a fair impression of what the term casual labour really meant in a pre-mechanised industry.

Coalheaving was the process of unloading the ships which had brought cargoes of coal from Newcastle to the Pool of London. If the collier moored in the middle of the river the coal was unloaded into a barge or lighter in which it was then taken to the wharf. The men who unloaded this cargo were called coalwhippers. But if the ship was able to tie up alongside the wharf, or alongside other barges moored to the wharf, the coal was unloaded directly on to the land and lightering was avoided. This process was known as coalbacking. The coalwhippers 'whipped' the coal out of the hold on to the deck and then overboard into the waiting barge. To do this they were organised in gangs of nine – eight whippers and a basket man or foreman. Four whippers in the hold filled a basket which held $1\frac{1}{4}$ cwt of coal; four others then hoisted it swiftly up 20 to 30 feet; and the basket man, balanced on a plank across the hold, swung it over the side into the weighing machine. A normal day's work was to whip (unload) 98 tons, though as much as 150 to 200 tons were sometimes unloaded. The price paid for whipping was 8d a ton which enabled the whippers to earn 15s to 20s for five days' work per week. But the work was irregular, so that earnings averaged over the year were much less. Until 1843 coalwhippers were organised and paid by public house keepers in the neighbourhood of the river from Tower Hill to Limehouse. Whippers were hired and paid in the pubs, and the purchase of drink was a condition of being 'taken on' for the day's work. In 1843 legislation was passed forbidding this system and substituting regulation and registration under the direction of commissioners.

Coalbacking was an even more strenuous job than whipping. Under this arrangement the coal was carried in sacks on the backs of the labourers from the hold of the ship to waggons on the wharf. The coalbacker carried his load up a ladder some 16 to 20 feet high from the hold to the deck, then along planks laid across four or five barges, and finally heaved it into the waggon. Each load weighed 2 cwt of coal plus 14 to 20 lbs for the sack, making 238 lbs in all. The men were organised in gangs of five (two shovelmen and three backers) and each gang was paid $11\frac{1}{4}$d per ton. About 30 to 40 tons would be unloaded in a day, for which each backer might receive 6s. 'Strong, hearty men' were said to make 25s to 30s a week, but since earnings during the slack summer season fell off, the average for the year was about 20s a week. Few men could survive this heavy labour for many years. Overstrain and accidents took a steady toll, and 'after a man turns forty he is considered to be past his work'. Even strong men could not keep at the work for more than two or three days consecutively, and had to hire unemployed mates to take their places. Coalheavers were prodigious drinkers for the work induced excessive thirst.

The perspiration in the summer time streams down our foreheads so rapidly that it will often get into our eyes before we have time to wipe it off. This makes the eyes very sore. At night, when we get home, we cannot bear to sit with a candle.

The same coalwhipper went on:

The thirst produced by our work is very excessive; it is completely as if you had a fever upon you. The dust gets into the throat, and very nearly suffocates you. You can scrape the coal dust off the tongue with the teeth; and do what you will it is impossible to get the least spittle into the mouth. I have known the coal dust to be that thick in a ship's hold that I have been unable to see my mate, though he was only two feet from me.[15]

The temperance cause made heavy weather in such a community. A coalbacker of twelve years' standing confessed that he limited himself to two pots of beer a day, 'that is, when I'm all day at work', though 'when times was better I drank fifteen pots a week'. As he explained to Mayhew:

I'll tell you what it is, Sir. Our work's harder than people guess at, and one must rest sometimes. Now if you sit down to rest without something to refresh you, the rest does you harm instead of good, for your joints seem to stiffen; but a good pull at a pot of beer backs

1 Barrow runs in the Tring cutting of the London and Birmingham Railway, opened 1837–38

2 Building the retaining wall, Camden Town, on the London and Birmingham Railway, 1837–38

3 Construction work on the tunnel at Edgehill, Liverpool and Manchester
Railway

4 Loading 'dollies' with a crane in a Durham coal mine, 1830s

5 Manual labour in the London docks. Ballast heavers at work

6 Coal heaving

7 Store vats at Barclay and
Perkins Brewery, South-
wark, 1847

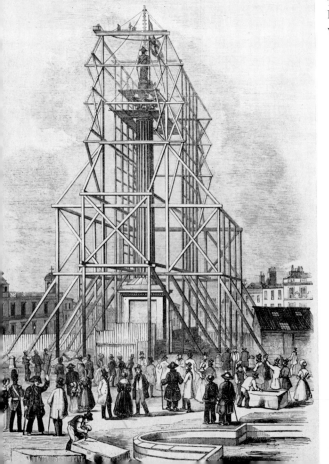

8 Erection of Nelson's
column, Trafalgar Square,
London, 1843

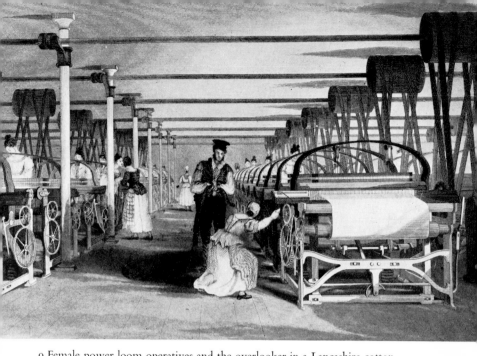

9 Female power loom operatives and the overlooker in a Lancashire cotton factory, 1835

10 Women and children at work in a cotton mill, 1835

11, 12 Field labour by men and women agricultural workers, 1846

13 Corn merchants at the Corn Exchange, Mark Lane, London, 1842

14 The Cockney grocer at home. Mr John Jorrocks of Great Coram Street and his assistant, Benjamin

15 Off to the races. Derby Day, 1844

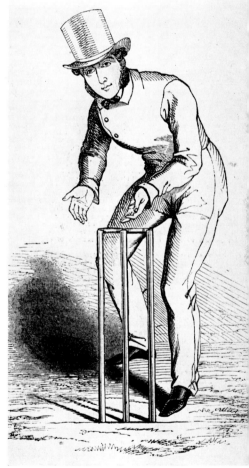

16, 17 Two celebrities of the cricket field, Messrs Pilch (16) and Box (17), 1843

18, 19 Two varieties of Easter Monday entertainment for Londoners, 1847: on the River Thames (18) and on Blackheath (19)

20 The Lord Mayor's procession at Ludgate Hill, London, November 1843

21 The Crystal Palace portrayed as the great hive of the world, 1851

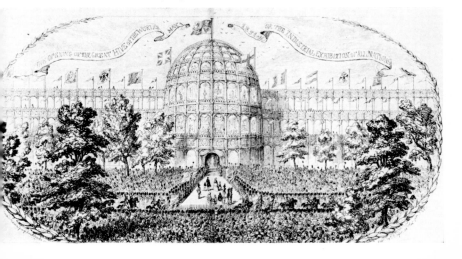

22 Improvement by example: 'look on this picture and on this'

23 Female influence

24 Visiting the Poor

25, 26 Two perennial subjects for middle class humour: servants and the Irish

"Are you not Irish?"
"Och no Ma'am, I'm Cornwall sure!"

"It's my Cousin Ma'am!"

27 The Royal family: Christmas tree at Windsor Castle

28 Making the Christmas
pudding

29 Eating it, in a middle class home

30 Working people taking home their Christmas dinners from a bakery

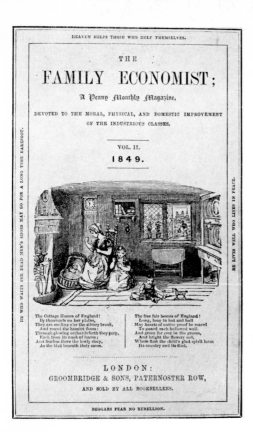

31 Improvement for the working classes

32 Culinary art, 1849

up the rest, and we start lightsomer. Our work's very hard. I've worked till my head's ached like to split; and when I've got to bed, I've felt as if I've had the weight on my back still ... feeling as if something was crushing my back flat to my chest.

He described how in summer 'the sweat's run into my boots', and how sometimes the strain made men bleed at the nose and mouth:

Sometimes we put a bit of coal in our mouths to prevent our biting our tongues ... but its almost as bad as if you did bite your tongue, for when the strain comes heavier and heavier on you, you keep scrunching the coal to bits, and swallow some of it, and you're half choked.[16]

The coal labourers in the metropolis numbered about five thousand men. This of course was only a part of the longshore population. Ballast men, corn labourers, stevedores, lumpers and riggers, timber labourers, bargemen and lightermen, and general dock labourers made up the rest of the labour force. Each section had its own customs, attractions, petty tyrannies and sufferings. But all were part of an army of unskilled labourers whose re-muneration was seldom much above subsistence level. Their role was well put by Mayhew: 'such a labourer, commercially con-sidered, is, as it were, a human steam-engine, supplied with so much fuel in the shape of food, merely to set him in motion'. Early Victorian Britain still relied more on the living than on the iron steam-engine.

Another large section of labouring people whose work has today been largely eliminated by mechanisation and greater efficiency was the domestic servants. In 1851 they totalled more than one million, and were the most numerous group of em-ployed persons after agriculture. Their work was in no sense as arduous as that of industrial or outdoor labourers, but it was continual, tiring and often monotonous; and the financial rewards were low. What could be said in favour of all the cease-less fetching and carrying and emptying, brushing, polishing, scrubbing, dusting, cooking, waiting, answering calls, feeding, nursing, washing-up – which had to be performed, day in day

C

out, in thousands of middle class homes throughout the land? The very design of a Victorian villa, tall and narrow, with the family sandwiched in between the servants' work area in the basement and their sleeping quarters in the attic, is a visible reminder of the expendability of human muscle in the cause of comfort. A majority of domestic servants were women: ladies' maids, house maids and parlour maids, cooks and scullery maids, nursery maids and wet nurses, dairy maids, maids of all work, charwomen and washerwomen. The men served as butlers, valets, footmen, pages, hall porters, coachmen, grooms, gardeners, boot boys and oddjob men. In public institutions, hotels and eating houses there were further opportunities for this type of work. A growing demand for personal service was one of the earliest signs of middle class prosperity. Perhaps no group was more taken for granted, less enquired into, and, on the rare occasions when it was noticed, treated with condescending humour. A steady supply of fresh domestic servants had to be maintained, for the turnover was high in an occupation staffed heavily with girls and young women who shortly left to get married. The recruits came from the surrounding country districts or were the daughters of respectable labouring men in the towns.

One distinctive element among the labouring poor was found in all the unskilled groups so far mentioned. The Irish immigrants living in Great Britain in 1841 were estimated to be about 400,000. Engels stated that over a million had emigrated to Britain, and that they were coming over at the rate of 50,000 a year. In Manchester and Liverpool they formed between a third and a fifth of the labouring population, and in London and the industrial towns they congregated thickly. They entered the depressed industries like handloom weaving, worked as casual labourers in agricultural districts, and undertook the heaviest jobs on the docks and railways. Everywhere they were ready to accept the jobs with the lowest pay, the longest hours or the toughest physical demands. Their miserable living conditions and apparently low expectations became notorious, and were documented in every government and local investigation of the 1840s. Engels' indignant account of the Irish in Manchester is a catalogue of phrases such as 'uncouth, improvident and addicted to drink', 'incredibly filthy conditions', and 'coarseness which drags him down virtually to the level of a savage'. He saw them as a threat to English workers: 'they are competitors whose standard of living is the lowest conceivable in a civilised country and consequently they are able to work for lower wages than anyone else'.

There is however another side to Engels' picture of 'the dissolute, volatile and drunken Irish'. Assimilation into an English or Scots working class community is not easy for immigrants, as West Indians and Pakistanis have discovered in recent times. The Irish were distinguished by their brogue, their Catholicism and their rural habits ('the Irishman loves his pig as much as the Arab loves his horse'), as well as by their clothes and physical appearance. If at times they appeared to be feckless, quick-tempered and prone to violence, it was also admitted that they were good-humoured, cheerful and long-suffering. Employers praised their loyalty and capacity for hard work. The Irish immigrant had a good deal of hostility to overcome. In addition to the xenophobia of English working men there was also an ancient tradition of anti-papism. Although the Irish labourer did not display many of the respectable virtues of thrift, sobriety and self-help, he was not significantly different in this respect from many of his English fellow navvies or coalheavers. Moreover, it was observed that when Irish immigrants had some strong motivation for saving, such as sending back a remittance to a family in Ireland, or accumulating the price of an emigrant ticket to America, they were perfectly capable of exercising the best puritan virtues. By the end of the nineteenth century the Irish who remained in Britain (for many immigrants used it only as a stage on the way to America) were absorbed into local working class communities. In the 1830s and 1840s they constituted an alien element within the labouring poor.

The categories enumerated so far comprised the bulk of the labouring population, but there were others. London had a large number of petty street traders, who differed from their middle class counterparts in that they did not have a shop but brought their wares to the consumer. The costermongers alone were estimated to number 30,000. All large cities had numbers of men employed as dustmen, scavengers, crossing sweepers, and lamplighters. The railways needed thousands of unskilled labourers for repair and maintenance work. And then there were the armed forces: the army had 41,000 men at home in 1841 and nearly 90,000 abroad. The navy and merchant marine numbered over 200,000 men. All these labouring men, whatever their earnings, status or degree of skill, were those who would (and for the most part did) work. There were also those who could not and would not work.

One of the defining characteristics of a labouring man was that he might involuntarily find himself in a condition where he could not work, and at any given time in the 1830s and 1840s a large number of the labouring poor were in this condition. The reasons for this were many but the most common one was that their labour was no longer required. They were, as we should now say, unemployed, though contemporaries (their minds dominated by Malthusian ideas of overpopulation) usually talked of surplus or redundant labour. The concept of continuous employment at all times for all labouring men was probably quite alien to most early Victorians: indigency, to a greater or lesser degree, was an acceptable (and inevitable) part of the lot of the lower orders. How widespread unemployment was in the period 1830–50 is extremely difficult to determine, though there are plenty of pieces of partial evidence. Certainly it was sufficiently acute to arouse alarm and investigation by the more fortunate sections of society. The Poor Law returns for 1844 showed that nearly 1½ million persons (or 9·3 per cent of the total population) had been relieved as paupers, either in the workhouse or outside.

National figures do not bring home the extent and intensity of unemployment so vividly as local examples. Take the case of Leeds. In the autumn of 1841 an Operative Enumeration Committee investigated the extent of distress through unemployment in the town. The committee claimed, on the basis of personal visitation, that out of 4,752 families examined, consisting of 19,936 individuals, only 3,780 persons were in work. Three months later 16,000 persons were receiving relief from the work-house, which meant that every fifth person in the township was a pauper. At each trade depression – in 1831, 1837, 1841–2, 1847–8 – unemployment became widespread. Again in April 1848, 15,000 persons were receiving relief from public soup kitchens. The devastating effects of unemployment on the conditions of work-ing class life will be considered later. The point to be made here is that the unemployed were so numerous and so constant that they have to be classified not as an exception but as a separate, though changing and fluctuating, category of the labouring poor.

Unemployment was not confined to periods of economic depression. It seems probable that in some parts of the economy there was a continual state of semi-employment, or concealed unemployment. Mayhew's researches led him to believe that only about a third of the labouring people in the country were fully employed, another third were partially employed, and the re-maining third wholly unemployed at any given time. He came to the conclusion that a great many jobs were in fact not full time but casual labour, and he ascribed this chiefly to 'a superfluity of labourers'. Unemployment, or casual labour was also created by other factors beyond the control of the worker. First and fore-most was the weather. Wet days deprived thousands of brick-layers, painters, agricultural labourers, and street sellers of their means of livelihood. An easterly wind prevailing for a few days spelled no work for 20,000 dock labourers in the Port of London. The effect of the seasons was to create brisk and slack periods in many trades: the coalwhippers had little work in summer, the bricklayers little in the winter. Fashion seasons also made brisk periods (February to July) followed by slack ones for tailors, boot and shoemakers, milliners, and such workers who depended on the demands of prosperous customers.

If a labouring man survived the hazards of unemployment – and even if he did not – there were two further ways in which he could join the category of those who could not work: by sickness and by old age. The risk of injury at work was high. Miners, navvies, dock workers and building trades labourers could expect to become casualties in the industrial army any day. Aches and pains, bronchitis and rheumatism afflicted agricultural labourers, whose clothes were often wet through for days on end. Unfenced machinery in the mills caused frightful mutilation of factory operatives: fingers crushed and limbs torn off. Employers accepted no liability for industrial injury. The most that labouring people could expect from them was a token payment for a serious accident or a few charitable gestures if they were 'laid up' for a longish spell. Sickness of the breadwinner immediately cut off the family's income, and unless the wife and children could find employment they were all plunged into pauperdom. An extension of credit at the local grocer's and steady use of the pawnshop might tide them over for a few weeks; but after that there was no recourse but to the guardians and the workhouse. Only the élite artisans were in a position to put anything by 'for a rainy day'. They alone had the support of sickness and unemployment benefits from their trade societies. Other groups such as the navvies and coalheavers had rudimentary sickness funds and voluntary collections for unfortunate mates, but only a limited number of cases could be taken care of in this way.

Finally, when a labouring man turned the age of fifty (and in heavy jobs much earlier) his strength and quickness began to desert him:

Most operatives in this country prematurely sink from labour, if they be not destroyed by acute disease [observed Dr Thackrah, a Leeds physician] 'Worn out' is as often applied to a workman as a coach-horse, and frequently with equal propriety in reference to premature decay.[17]

A coalbacker aged forty-five confessed that after twenty-two years on the job he had had to give it up because he had 'overstrained' himself, and that now he was virtually finished. Old age was anything but a pleasant anticipation of retirement for a labouring man. With no provision for an income, unable to continue with his job, and in failing health, the most he could hope for himself and his wife was a corner by the fireside in his children's home in return for such odd jobs and baby minding as they could manage. If this were not available the only place for them to go was the workhouse.

The last category of labouring folk were those who would not work. In adopting this categorisation Mayhew was not giving vent to a private moral judgement, but voicing the informed contemporary view that vagrants and criminals formed a separate section of the labouring poor, with its own distinctive attitudes and behaviour. Crime was an occupation for this group in the same way that cabinet-making or coalheaving was for others. The notion that crime, particularly theft, was committed casually by workers who were reduced to indigency was not supported by most enquirers:

Having investigated the general causes [of crime and vagrancy, reported the Constabulary Commissioners in 1839] we find that scarcely in any cases is it ascribable to the pressure of unavoidable want or destitution, and that in the great mass of cases it arises from the temptation of obtaining property with a less degree of labour than by regular industry.[18]

A young pickpocket, relating his experiences of thieving to John Binny, one of Mayhew's assistants, talked about how he was 'generally employed working in the streets', 'did not work at ladies' pockets', and at one stage in his career 'barely kept myself in respectability'. Such men were specialists, members of a distinct group whose trade was crime.

The world of those who would not work, like other sections of the labouring poor, was very consciously hierarchical. At the bottom of the heap were the vagrants. Vagrancy was no new problem. Since the sixteenth century the state had fiercely tried to suppress 'sturdy idle rogues and vagabonds', but with indifferent success. By the 1840s there was a regular body of nomads who frequented the casual wards of the workhouses. The tattered figure of the regular tramp was for many years to come a familiar figure by the English roadside: today he has all but disappeared. Why men became vagrants is not altogether clear. Victorians offered a psychological explanation ('love of idleness') and also suggested socio-economic factors of unfavourable environment ('non-inculcation of a habit of industry'). Some vagrants may have been unemployed artisans or labourers who set out 'on tramp' to look for work but, finding none, remained to become wandering mendicants. Others were run-away apprentices, neglected youths from large towns, immigrant Irishmen, anyone who had an 'impatience of steady labour'. It was noticed that a majority of the vagrants were between fifteen and twenty-five. How many there were is impossible to calculate accurately: estimates varied from 40,000 to 100,000 for England and Wales.

That vagrancy was the nursery of crime was accepted as axiomatic: habitual tramps became first beggars, then thieves and finally convicts. Today a beggar is a rare sight in England, and a whole generation has grown up scarcely knowing what the term means. In early Victorian Britain beggars were ubiquitous, ingenious and colourful. The streets of London and the large towns contained a whole section of the population who lived by soliciting alms from passers-by. Some claimed to be ex-sailors and army veterans who had deserved well of their country. Others said they were distressed operatives, decayed gentlemen, ship-wrecked mariners, blown-up miners, or burnt-out tradesmen. There were beggars who paraded their children, showed real or pretended sores, or exhibited themselves half-clad in cold weather in order to arouse pity. The blind, crippled, maimed and paralysed displayed themselves. Some called attention to their condition, others stood mutely with a placard saying 'I am starving'. There were 'artists' who chalked on the pavement, and sellers of matches and bootlaces. They were of all ages and of both sexes. Their object was to trade on the consciences of others more fortunate than themselves.

Beggars as a group were separate from habitual criminals, though the younger and more active beggars might well progress into the lower branches of crime. Among the aristocrats of the criminal world were the cracksmen (housebreakers and burglars) and the high class pickpockets known as mobsmen. Thieving was a very specialised job: the stealing of a gentleman's handkerchief by a buzzer, for instance, required a different technique from thimble-screwing (stealing a pocket watch). Shop-lifting was regarded as a skilled and lucrative craft. Less prestigious (and less remunerative) were the sneaksmen, thieves who robbed tills in shops, stole goods and luggage from carts and coaches, or took goods displayed outside shops. Then there were horse-stealers, embezzlers, and forgers; and of course the important fences or receivers of stolen goods. Thieving had its customs and regulations like any other craft. A rough apprenticeship began at the age of six or seven, when, as a ragged urchin, the young thief tried his hand at petty pilfering. He vied with his fellows as to who could excel, and did not consider that what he was doing was either unusual or wrong. From stealing oranges off stalls he soon moved on to more difficult jobs, and with some advice and training from adult criminals he graduated to the ranks of the sneaksmen and, if he were lucky, might become a swell mobsman. Experienced burglars would sometimes use a boy as an accomplice, as Bill Sykes used Oliver in Dickens' novel, *Oliver Twist*. As with other trades, criminals tended to live in certain districts of large towns, though they usually operated elsewhere. Hours of work were determined by the nature of the job. Early morning was a good time for sneaksmen, as shopkeepers were then putting their goods on display outside and servants were opening up homes and occupied with their chores. The dusk of the evening was a busy time for pickpockets, and indeed for all types of thieves. For burglary and housebreaking night work was almost obligatory. High class jobs were usually done by a gang, with each member deputed to look after one aspect of the operation.

Thieves' earnings are extremely difficult to estimate. One day a pickpocket might make a great deal and the next almost nothing. The top members of the profession apparently were able to live at a middle class standard, enjoying fashionable clothes, supporting a woman of their own, and going to the theatre and smart eating houses. However these prosperous periods were interrupted by longish spells in prison. Any day the thief might be caught and then 'lagged' for six months or longer. After a number of such convictions he was liable to transportation for a further offence: as a result the attrition rate in the criminal population was high.

Between 1810 and 1852 some 140,000 persons were transported to Australia, the overwhelming majority for theft. Most criminals lived with their flashgirl or mistress. She was usually an accomplice in thieving as well as a prostitute, and the interconnection between theft and prostitution was close. We shall not at present examine the role of prostitution in early Victorian society: suffice it to note that prostitutes formed yet another group within the world of those who would not work, and that they too had their hier-archy of status and earnings, their trade customs and their aspirations.

How large was this section of the population who had such a rooted aversion to 'steady labour', this world of criminals and their hangers-on which seems so remote from the experiences of most readers of this book? It is almost impossible to say. The best evidence that we have is little more than inspired guesswork. Mayhew estimated that the number of thieves in the metropolis was 12,000 to 15,000, and that the entire criminal population of England and Wales was about 150,000. But Mayhew was often careless with his statistics and the basis of his computation may be unreliable. The most we can be sure of is that this underworld of crime was well known to the early Victorians and that they regarded it as a distinct and permanent section of the lower orders.

We return then to the point made earlier in this chapter, that the labouring poor, who comprised all but a small minority of the British people, were such a large and complex body that they cannot usefully be generalised about as a whole. They have to be treated as a series of social groups or sub-classes. Nevertheless all these groups (including the criminals) possessed certain features in common. They were all dependent on the labour of their hands and bodies for their livelihood, and even their most highly rewarded members received no more than was sufficient for a modest degree of comfort. The majority had very few of this world's goods. In fact the social structure we have been describing was essentially a pattern of poverty.

3
The Condition-of-England
Question

'A feeling very generally exists,' wrote the prophet of the early Victorian age, Thomas Carlyle, in 1839, 'that the condition and disposition of the Working Classes is a rather ominous matter at present; that something ought to be said, something ought to be done, in regard to it.'[1] Carlyle was reacting to the 'bitter discontent grown fierce and mad', expressed in Chartism and opposition to the New Poor Law, and he voiced the widespread concern about the economic and social plight of the labouring poor. This concern was both a cause and a result of many investigations into living and working conditions in the 1830s and 1840s. No previous age had been so much enquired into by select committees, royal commissions, statistical societies and local bodies, nor had there been such a spate of bluebooks (government publications) and reports by amateur investigators. Documentation of the condition-of-England question was very thorough.

But contemporaries were divided in their interpretations of these facts, and consequently also in their views as to what 'ought to be done'. Historians likewise have differed among themselves for many years on this issue. The debate has been between those who took an optimistic view of the new industrial civilisation and those whose verdict was pessimistic. Dr Andrew Ure in his *Philosophy of Manufactures* (1835), and G.R.Porter, quoted earlier, regarded the industrial changes as a blessing; Carlyle and Engels saw them as a curse. More recently the issues have been narrowed down by historians to an argument as to whether the standard of living of the working classes improved or deteriorated between 1780 and 1850. No very clear conclusion has so far emerged, perhaps because of failure to agree on standards of measurement. Statistics of earnings and prices, unemployment, patterns of consumption (including food), and population growth have all been introduced as variables in assessing changes in working class living standards. Even more difficult to ascertain is firm information about the qualitative aspects of life of the labouring poor; for here there is almost no escape from personal judgements, whether by contemporaries or historians. If a general statement about the material condition of the working classes during the Industrial Revolution were to be hazarded, it would be that the real income of skilled artisans increased, the lot of the domestic workers deteriorated, and the living standards of the majority of the labouring poor remained stationary or at best improved slightly. During the crucial second quarter of the nineteenth century even this cautious evaluation may be disputed. So fluctuating was the economy in booms and slumps, so widespread the incidence of unemployment, and so low the living standards of the eight million inhabitants of Ireland, that generalisation becomes meaningless. It is clear that large numbers, possibly a majority, of the labouring poor suffered an absolute decline in living standards during the 1830s and 1840s, and that the working class as a whole declined relative to other groups in their share of the national income. From the late forties improvement began, and continued until late in the century. In early Victorian Britain there were as yet few indications of this later development.

Although comparison of standards of living at different periods is difficult, description of living conditions in the 1830s and 1840s is less so. We know a fair amount about the sort of homes people lived in, the food they ate and the clothes they wore. We can say something about their habits at work and at home, their attitudes and assumptions and routines. We can even guess at some of their hopes and aspirations, though here we are faced with the monumental obstacle that the vast majority of the labouring poor were normally inarticulate. They had few spokesmen of their own, and their case was only occasionally presented by sympathisers from the middle class.

Smile at us, pay us, pass us, but do not quite forget.
For we are the people of England, that never has spoken yet.[2]

The condition-of-England question was not the labourer's statement of his condition but the formulation of a 'problem' by critics of early Victorian society drawn from the more literate classes. Nevertheless this focusing of attention on certain aspects of the social life of the labouring poor provided a more complete picture than had ever been obtained previously.

'As the homes, so the people,' argued Victorian housing reformers (unintentionally substantiating Robert Owen's doctrine of circumstances). The people, as we have seen, were far from homogeneous, and it is therefore rather misleading to think of a particular type of home – whether in Little Ireland (Manchester), Spitalfields, or a Dorset village – as typical of the labouring poor. Contemporaries, as always, tended to describe the very best and the very worst, and omitted details of the norm, which they took for granted. In general, most urban and some rural workers lived in cottages of three or four rooms and a kitchen. Such homes were two-storeyed, and (in the towns) were built in terraces or around courts. Unlike the labouring poor on the Continent, very few British workers lived in tenements: only in the old town of Edinburgh were there to be found tenement buildings up to ten storeys high. British towns expanded outwards rather than upwards. Long rows of terrace houses in red brick, or sometimes of stone in the northern towns, sprawled outwards from the older city centres. Having first filled up all available space within the existing town, they snaked across the surrounding hills or clustered near the factories in the valley bottoms. In the medieval town (the relics of which had survived into the eighteenth century) rich and poor, merchants and labourers, had been more or less intermingled, but in the nineteenth century the labouring poor became segregated in exclusively working class districts.

In Leeds, for instance, the statistical committee of the town council in 1839 estimated that of the total population of 82,120 in the township, 61,212 belonged to the working classes, and the majority of these lived in certain well-defined areas of the town. The North, North East and Kirkgate wards, together with the rapidly growing out-townships of Holbeck and Hunslet formed a densely populated working class area; while the middle classes occupied the healthier and more pleasantly situated areas in the Mill Hill, West, and North West wards. The sorting out of the population into different areas on a basis of social status was thus far advanced, and the social distinctions between the working classes and their more affluent neighbours, already apparent in differences of dress, speech, and mental attitudes, was reinforced by physical isolation. The gulf between classes inevitably widened, and to many social reformers the bridging of this gulf seemed the most urgent and yet most difficult task of all.

Within this warren of working class housing in Leeds there was a big variation between the best and the worst. The homes of respectable working men usually rented for 2s 6d to 7s 6d a week. In 1839 there were 8,331 houses rented at between £5 and £10 per year, and a further 2,640 at between £10 and £20. The cheapest of these houses consisted of two rooms and a cellar, built back to back, and sharing an outside privy. Describing such cottages in the 1850s, Edward Hall, the Unitarian Domestic Missionary in Holbeck, emphasised the details of daily life in such accommodation:

They are built back to back, with no possibility of good ventilation, and contain a cellar for coals and food, the coal department being frequently tenanted with fowls, pigeons, or rabbits, and in some cases with two or all three of these – a room from 9 to 14 feet by from 10 to 12 or 14 feet, to do all the cooking, washing, and the necessary work of a family, and another of the same size for all to sleep in. Think for a moment what must be the inconvenience, the danger both in a moral and physical sense, when parents and children, young men and women, married and single, are crowded together in this way, with three beds in a room, and barely a couple of yards in the middle for the whole family to undress and dress in.[3]

Taking further Hall's invitation to consider the implications of such housing, it is not difficult to imagine some of the rawer aspects of working class life in the home: the lack of indoor sanitation and consequent use of chamber pots; the absence of a water tap in the house and the difficulties of keeping personally clean; the aggravation of these problems by an aged and incontinent relative or by a sick person; the difficulty of ever airing the house because through ventilation was made impossible by the back-to-back construction. Even in the better cottages with two bedrooms ('two up and two down') these problems were mitigated but not removed. And while there was little enough room for the family indoors, there was even less outside in the way of garden or yard. The houses opened directly on to the street, with the result that:

the intersection of the street with clothes-lines is an anomaly in street regulations. In the township of Leeds, out of the total number of 586 streets, 276, or nearly one-half are weekly so full of lines and linen as to be impassable for horses and carriages, and almost for foot-passengers.[4]

Skilled artisans enjoyed considerably more comfort at home. Their cottages were larger, in more salubrious areas of the town, and usually had a small yard at the back. The windows were often well-proportioned, and the doorways showed traces of simple Regency elegance. Today such terraces of artisans' and lower middle class houses can still be found in most towns, and in Chelsea and Islington are much sought after for fashionable 'doing up'. Inside the furnishings were usually described as comfortable, meaning something beyond the basic necessities of bed, table and chairs. Such things as clocks, pictures, books, ornaments, floor coverings, oak or mahogany chests of drawers were taken as signs of decency and prosperity. And if a parlour, separate from the everyday living room could be maintained, then respectability was assured. Standards of housewifery were high, with much emphasis on scrubbing and scouring and polishing (the custom of whitening door steps and window sills in northern towns persists to this day). Nowhere did the great Victorian virtues of frugality, cleanliness and sobriety appear more attractively and to greater purpose than in 'the cottage homes of

England'. They provided the inspiration for dozens of building societies, model cottage societies and improved dwellings associations: for, it was argued, what some members of the working class had achieved all should be encouraged to strive for.

Both the need and the difficulties of such improvement were amply demonstrated at the other extreme. The worst housing conditions were the slums of the big towns, and in particular the cellar dwellings and common lodging houses. Engels, in his *Condition of the Working Class in England in 1844*, described in vivid detail the squalor of the cellar dwellings in Manchester, of which there were 20,000 in 1832. The same story was repeated in Glasgow, London, Liverpool and other industrial towns where there were immigrant Irish and handloom weavers. Robert Baker, a surgeon and factory inspector of Leeds, described local Irish cellar dwellings which he had visited:

I have been in one of these damp cellars, without the slightest drainage, every drop of wet and every morsel of dirt and filth having to be carried up into the street; two corded frames for beds, overlaid with sacks for five persons; scarcely anything in the room else to sit on but a stool, or a few bricks; the floor, in many places, absolutely wet; a pig in the corner also; and in a street where filth of all kinds had accumulated for years. In another house, where no rent had been paid for years by reason of apparent inability to do it, I found a father and mother and their two boys, both under the age of sixteen years, the parents sleeping on similar corded frames, and the two boys upon straw, on the floor upstairs; never changing their clothes from week's end to week's end, working in the dusty department of a flax mill, and existing upon coffee and bread.[5]

There is all too much evidence from the 1830s to make it clear that this report was neither exaggerated nor untypical. In the area of Greater Manchester there was a total of 40,000 to 50,000 people living in cellars, in Liverpool more than 45,000. The evil arose from the subdivision of what had been intended as a home for a single family into a series of tenements with each room occupied by one or even more families, the cheapest and most undesirable room being the cellar, which was below street level and lighted only by a grating.

Equally sordid conditions were found in many of the dwellings in courts and alleys which were above ground. In some cases older and larger houses had been broken down into single-room dwellings. But more frequently cottages were built round a court entered by a narrow alley from the street. In London the districts of Seven Dials and Bethnal Green, in Glasgow the Wynds, in Manchester the old town, in Leeds the Kirkgate ward, all contained examples of this type of housing. Sites in the central areas of towns were at a premium and there was every encouragement to build as many houses as possible per acre. In York and Leeds the courts were built in what had been the gardens of older and more spacious homes: in Nottingham and Coventry overcrowded 'rookeries' were created by the shortage of building land consequent upon the refusal to enclose the common lands which hemmed in the town. Lodging houses were usually found in these areas and were particularly noisome and notorious as the haunts of beggars, tramps, thieves and prostitutes. A report on lodging houses in Leeds was prepared by the police in 1851 after an outbreak of typhus fever had been traced to some of the lodgers.[6] Within a half-circle drawn at a radius of a quarter of a mile from the parish church were found 222 lodging houses, 53 of them being in Wellington Yard alone. Nearly 2,500 people lived in these lodgings, averaging $2\frac{1}{2}$ persons to each bed and $4\frac{1}{2}$ persons to each room. In one house there were ten persons per bed. Men and women slept indiscriminately together in the same room in 220 of the 222 houses. The charge for lodging was 2d to 3d per night. Only 40 of the 220 houses were even moderately clean, and six were cellar dwellings in a filthy condition.

The inadequacy of private dwellings was matched by the paucity of social provision of utilities and amenities. Edwin Chadwick, more than any other single person, aroused his countrymen to an awareness of the 'sanitary condition' of England, but it was only gradually and reluctantly that municipalities accepted the duty of providing a minimum of basic services. The early Victorian town was still largely unpaved, unsewered, ill-lit and inadequately supplied with clean water. Working class housing areas were nearly always in the low lying parts of the town in what had previously been meadows and marshes along the banks of a river – precisely those areas in which efficient sewerage and drainage was at once the most necessary and yet the most difficult to construct. In 1839 in the North East ward of Leeds, containing a working class population of over 15,000, only three streets were wholly, and twelve partly sewered out of a total of 93. It was a common habit in the poorest areas to empty chamber pots in the street. Even when privies were provided, if they could not be flushed into a sewer, the contents had to be periodically dug out and carted away. Investigators commented frequently on the disgusting smells and 'excrementitious matter' lying about in all directions. An equally small number of streets was paved; the rest were simply beaten earth. In Leeds ashes were sometimes laid down to form a pavement, which in dry weather produced an irritating black dust and on wet days a spongey black puddle. Only in the superior type of artisan's cottage was water laid on. In the normal back to back terrace house water had to be drawn from a common tap in the yard or on the privy wall.

The health hazard from such conditions was only tardily admitted. There was a strange reluctance to accept the idea of a causal relationship between the incidence of disease and the effectiveness of the sanitation system. But typhus fever, cholera and smallpox were no respecters of persons. Although the diseases usually originated amongst, and ravaged most severely the very poorest of the labouring classes, they inevitably took their toll of all sections of the people living in the congested areas of the town. It was Robert Baker who, from the time of his first report on the Leeds cholera epidemic of 1832, showed repeatedly how epidemic disease and high mortality rates clung to the working class areas. Chadwick's *Report on the Sanitary Condition of the Labouring Population of Great Britain*, put the matter succinctly:

By the inspection of a map of Leeds, which Mr Baker has prepared at my request, to show the localities of epidemic diseases, it will be perceived that they similarly fall on the uncleansed and close streets and wards occupied by the labouring classes; and that the track of the cholera is nearly identical with the track of fever. It will also be observed that in the badly cleansed and badly drained wards to the right of the map, the proportional mortality is nearly double that which prevails in the better conditioned districts to the left.[7]

Despite such convincing reports it was long before municipal authorities could bring themselves to incur the cost of adequate sewerage for the whole of their towns.

In rural areas the living conditions of the labouring poor were not essentially different from those of comparable groups in the towns. Although lodging houses and cellar dwellings were absent from the villages, there were rural slums which were as squalid as anything in Manchester. The cottages of most farm labourers were no larger than those of town workers, though the general rural environment was perhaps less depressing than the smoky pall which hung over the low-lying centres of industrial towns. William Blades, an East Riding agricultural worker, was born in 1839 at Nafferton, a large village lying on the eastern side of the Wolds in the heart of a rich corn-growing district, and his account of his life there in the forties and fifties was set down many years later by a sympathetic country rector.

The house of the Blades family was, like all the houses of the agricultural labourers, small, consisting of two rooms on the ground floor called the 'house', or living room, and the parlour, with two bedrooms above. In many of the cottages at that time there was over one or other of the sleeping chambers a space or area, it could not be dignified with the title of room, which was frequently used as a sleeping-place for some of the children; it was just possible to get a small bed or two into it; and there they slept in their beds in the manner shortly to be described. So contracted was the space, that in getting out of bed the youngsters had to exercise great caution so as not to knock their heads against the rafters of the roof. This upper area always went by the name of 'cockloft'. . . . In addition to these rooms there was what was called a 'backer-end', which was a kind of lean-to shanty at one end of the house.[8]

The Blades' home may be taken as a fairly standard English rural cottage: a few (approaching small farmhouses) were better, but many were much worse. Regional variations accounted for some of the differences; thus in the Cotswolds and the West Riding the building was of stone, in Lancashire and the Midlands of brick. Older cottages were made of wattle and daub, and in some areas a half-timbered construction was used. Turf houses were still common in parts of Scotland, and of course were practically universal in Ireland. The amount of accommodation seldom exceeded the Blades' house, and in northern England and the Lowlands of Scotland there were one-roomed cottages, sometimes with animals living under the same roof and divided from the dwelling room by only a nominal partition wall. Floors were usually of brick, pebble or earth; furnishings were utilitarian; and privies were sometimes completely absent. Idyllic as many English cottages looked in summer, when they were embowered in honeysuckle and hollyhocks and roses, and superior as they undoubtedly were to rural homes in Ireland and on the Continent, life in such conditions did not leave much margin for comfort. The cottage afforded little more than the basic requirements of shelter, warmth and a place to eat.

Eating for the labouring poor was not the graceful social occasion that it was for some other classes. Despite romantic myths about plenty of roast beef, pudding and strong ale, the food of a majority of the people had always been very limited in amount and variety. By modern standards the traditional fare of our ancestors was stodgy, monotonous and nutritionally deficient. During the first half of the nineteenth century there is little firm evidence that this state of things improved, though there were some important dietary changes. Consumption of basic foods in this period did not rise appreciably, and during the depression years of the 1830s and early 1840s it declined. Only after the mid-forties did the consumption trend for most foods turn upwards. As with housing and other social indices, food was directly tied to income, and reflected the basic divisions within the working classes. The general situation was summed up by Engels:

The normal diet of the individual worker naturally varies according to his wages. The better-paid workers – particularly when the whole family works in the factories – enjoy good food as long as they are in employment. They have meat every day and bacon and cheese for the evening meal. The lower-paid workers have meat only two or three times a week, and sometimes only on Sundays. The less meat they can afford, the more potatoes and bread they eat. Sometimes the meat consumed is cut down to a little chopped bacon mixed with the potatoes. The poorer workers can afford no meat at all and they eat cheese, bread, porridge and potatoes. The poorest of all are the Irish, for whom potatoes are the staple diet. In addition, most workers drink weak tea to which perhaps sugar, milk, or spirits are added. In England and even in Ireland tea is regarded as being just as essential as coffee is in Germany and only those who suffer from the direst poverty give up their tea.

This was a description of town workers. But until the middle of the century their diet was not appreciably different from that of rural labourers. The Blades family breakfasted on brown or barley bread, treacle, water and an occasional 'sup' of milk. Because tea was too expensive to buy, the mother collected used tea leaves from the landlord of a neighbouring inn and used them over again. For dinner at mid-day there was broth obtained from a farm three days a week, mashed potatoes with pepper and salt, and sometimes dumplings. The evening meal was similar to breakfast, with the possible addition of a bit of cheesecake or apple pie. Almost everywhere in rural England the basic diet was bread, potatoes and tea, with bacon two or three times a week. Prosperity (which tended to increase the more northern the county) meant the addition of more meat, and also milk and cheese.

The dietary habits of early Victorian Britain were in certain respects significantly different from those of the eighteenth century. White bread and tea, which in pre-industrial society had been the luxuries of the upper classes, were by the 1830s staple fare of the labouring poor throughout the southern and midland counties and in the industrial towns. The universal use of the potato was also relatively new and occasioned Cobbett's disgust, for he was convinced that the spread of potato eating represented a degradation in the labourer's standard of living. Home baking and brewing – another of Cobbett's nostrums for labouring happiness – decayed rapidly after 1815, though in the North the tradition lingered longer than in the South. Domestic brewing required equipment, materials and fuel which few labourers could afford. Similarly with baking; where white bread could be had from the baker for a few pence, why should the labourer's wife go to the trouble and expense of baking her own?

Behind the rather unimaginative food habits of the labouring poor there was often a rationale that escaped the well-meaning, middle class dieticians who proffered their (largely disregarded) advice for improvement. In the cottages that we have described, with only an open fire or at best a primitive iron oven, how could the housewife do any elaborate cooking? If she worked in a factory or in the fields or helped her husband in a home craft she had little time left for food preparation. There was therefore a premium on those dishes which were at once tasty and quick to serve – anything which could be bought ready to eat (bread) or which could be boiled (potatoes, soup) or fried (bacon). The craving for 'something tasty' was satisfied in many ways, from the Blades' simple addition of salt and pepper to their potatoes, to the cotton operatives' preference for 'rusty' bacon. And always there was tea, the great standby of the English working classes down to the present day. Not all Cobbett's sneers could prevent the addiction to 'a nice cuppa tea' which made the dry bread and monotonous fare more palatable.

A glance at an actual budget will make clear how small was the margin for even an occasional 'extra' in the food line. With regular earnings of 15s a week a London labouring man in 1841 might just support himself, his wife and three children thus:[9]

	s	d
5 4lb loaves at 8½d	3	6½
5 lb meat at 5d	2	1
7 pints of porter at 2d	1	2
½ cwt coals		9½
40 lb potatoes	1	4
3 oz tea, 1 lb sugar	1	6
1 lb butter		9
½ lb soap, ½ lb candles		6½
Rent	2	6
Schooling		4
Sundries		5½

Apart from what this does not include (milk, cheese, fresh vegetables, clothing, shoes, provision for sickness) it postulates continuous employment, which was far from the lot of most labouring men. Even supposing the wife were also able to earn, it is difficult to see how such a family could escape periods of destitution. At times of trade depression they would simply not have enough to eat. Old men who later looked back on their childhood in the 1830s and 1840s recalled that they felt hungry almost all the time. That this was the condition of the Irish peasantry is well known; but it is probably no exaggeration to say that the majority of labouring people in Britain in the 1830s and early 1840s at some time went short of food. To lose a child because he could not provide it with adequate food (as was the fate of George Jacob Holyoake during his imprisonment for blasphemy in 1842) was the way that the iron entered into a man's soul. Even better-paid workers, who while they had work lived well, fell into semi-starvation when they were unemployed. The navvy had to forgo his steaks and ale when times were bad and he was laid off. In this respect the alternation of good and bad times, of feasting and fasting, was but another example of that continuation of pre-industrial living and working patterns noted earlier.

Two further factors have to be included in any assessment of the labouring man's food situation: adulteration and credit. The notion of adulterated food is so strange nowadays that most people find it hard to credit the difficulty which labouring people had in obtaining their basic foods in a pure condition. Ale and porter were treated with *cocculus indicus* (a dangerous poison) as a cheap substitute for malt and hops, and new beer had sulphuric acid added to make it taste mature. Bread contained a small quantity of alum whose purpose was to whiten an inferior grade of flour; and potatoes, chalk and pipe-clay were also used in so-called wheaten bread. Tea was adulterated in several ways, such as mixing with used tea leaves which had been treated with gum and dried, or adding 'British tea' made from dried and curled local leaves from the hedgerows. It was easy to add floor sweepings to pepper or to dilute milk with water. All these frauds were difficult for the ordinary consumer to detect, and he was thus at the mercy of the retailer who perpetrated them. When the modern consumers' cooperative movement was started at Rochdale in 1844, two of its objectives were to supply unadulterated food and avoid the clutches of the private shopkeeper. But for many years the insistence on cash trading limited the cooperatives to the better-off sections of the working class. A majority of the labouring poor could not exist without credit.

The small shopkeeper was an extremely important figure in working class life. He supplied the bread, groceries and household goods – all sold in small quantities to suit the pockets of the poor – and knew his customers intimately. In times of unemployment or sickness, or towards the end of the week when earnings were exhausted, he supplied goods on credit. Once in debt it was extremely difficult for a labouring family to get out, and a situation soon developed where future earnings were mortgaged ahead of time. This delivered the customer completely into the hands of the shopkeeper, who could force the acceptance of adulterated, inferior and over-priced goods. Cases of shopkeepers fined for using deficient weights and defective scales were common in the factory districts. The man who ran the little shop at the corner of the street did not have to be a villain in order to exploit his neighbours. The system whereby he made a living out of selling cheap goods in small quantities on extended credit inevitably ensured that the customer paid dearly in the long run. Similarly the ubiquitous pawnshop was the dearest, but ineluctable method of raising a short term loan. When Mayhew asked a meeting of coalwhippers how many of them had things in pawn, there was a general laugh and a cry of 'All of us'. It was common to pawn a coat on Monday and take it out on Saturday, paying a month's interest. One man said, 'I have now in pawn seven articles, all wearing apparel, my wife's or my own, from 15s down to 9d.[10] The procession to the pawnshop every Monday morning, the pledging of article after article as the week wore on, and the redemption on Saturday evening after wages had been paid, was a familiar part of working class life in all the large towns. Manchester had over sixty pawnshops in 1844 and in Salford one street alone had ten or twelve.

A form of credit which was particularly resented was truck, or the payment of wages in kind. This was traditional in some occupations, but that did not make it any the more acceptable. The employer kept a store or 'tommy shop' where his workers were required, or found it convenient to buy their provisions. In some instances wages were paid in food tickets redeemable only at the store. On railway construction work wages were not always paid weekly, but fortnightly or monthly, and credit was advanced against purchases in the tommy shop. The convenience of a store when working in remote areas was obvious, but the temptation to abuse was so overwhelming that the system was condemned by the navvies. 'At the tommy-shop we was charged half as much again as we should have had to pay elsewhere; and it's the same now, wherever these tommy shops is,' declared a navvy who had had eighteen years' experience of them.[11] There were instances of the tommy shops being run by a ganger or a man who had paid a commission for the concession, and when advances were paid in shop tickets he would allow cash for them at a discount. Coal miners and textile operatives in factory villages were also subject to payment in truck. The Midland framework knitters were notoriously burdened with it, and in times of depression other domestic outworkers, such as the Black Country nailmakers, could be forced to accept payment in truck. In the London docks until 1843 coalwhippers could only get work by spending as much as half of their earnings with the publicans who hired them. The ballast-heavers were obliged to lodge at the house of the foreman who hired them, and to spend their earnings at the grocer's, butcher's or publican's who had engaged the foreman and who contracted for ballasting the ships. Unmarried farm servants in the north of England who 'lived in' were paid very infrequently and a part of their wages was accounted for by board and lodging. Married farm labourers who occupied a 'rent free' tied cottage or received concessions to enable them to keep a pig had sometimes to accept these in lieu of cash payment for extra work done.

The losses to the labouring poor from truck, adulteration, unemployment, epidemic disease and squalor did not go unperceived by them and, as we shall see later, provoked fierce agitation in the 1830s. Dependence upon the tommy shopkeeper, the pawnbroker, and the landlord was resented as much as the actual economic or physical loss sustained. It meant the destruction of traditional ideas about independence, the family and just dealing in a society; it reduced the labouring man to something less than he had been and felt he had a right to be. When Peter Gaskell, a sympathetic doctor, Richard Oastler, the Yorkshire factory reformer, Karl Marx and Friedrich Engels used the words slavery and serfdom to describe this condition they were not being exaggeratedly dramatic but merely voicing a fairly common sentiment of the 1830s and 1840s. The feeling of not being one's own master even when not at work, of not having any effective choice in even the small things of life, was perhaps the most demoralising effect of the living conditions we have been describing. On a marginal or near-starvation budget there was no room for manoeuvre. Had the labourer and his wife been expert and disciplined spenders of their meagre and irregular income they would still have been hard pressed to make ends meet. The majority of labouring people were of course anything but efficient in this respect. Their traditional culture, rooted in the pre-industrial past, in no way equipped them for such tasks. Habits of Saint Monday, customary drinking usages, and slap-up funerals with a ham tea (all condemned by middle class sympathisers) made little sense in a society regulated by the 'cash nexus', as Carlyle put it. Partly the condition-of-England question was a painful adjustment to this new situation. Until the adjustment was made, an improvement in standards of living, despite increased earnings, was unlikely.

A conspicuous example of apparent failure to make the best use of available income was expenditure on drinking. Temperance workers assessed the total amount spent on drink at over £67 million in 1830 and nearly £81 million in 1850. This averaged nearly £3 per person per year, which in a labouring family of five or six amounted to more than they paid in rent. Here surely, argued the temperance reformers, was the explanation of the misery of the labouring poor and the secret of how to better their condition. Moreover the gross effects of drunkenness could be seen any Saturday night in any town in Britain, with labouring men staggering about or lying helpless in the gutter. After the Beerhouse Act of 1830, which permitted virtually any householder who paid a small fee to sell beer on his premises, the number of beerhouses (Tom and Jerry shops) increased by 30,000 to 40,000. Manchester had nearly a thousand inns, beer houses and gin shops, Leeds township some 450 in the 1830s. In Glasgow it was estimated that there was one public house to every ten dwelling houses in 1840, and that 30,000 persons were drunk every Saturday night. Illicit stills, often operated by Irish cellar dwellers, added further to the national consumption of alcohol. Gaskell thought that in Manchester alone the output from such stills was 156,000 gallons a year. It is difficult to know quite what to make of these rather staggering figures. Averaging them is probably futile, since they represent a series of different styles of living rather than one standard pattern. At one extreme were the coalheavers who had to spend part of their wages on drink as a condition of getting work, or the ironworkers, glass-blowers and navvies engaged in thirst-making occupations; at the other were some artisans and factory operatives who drank very little or were teetotal. However, where drinking was common, whether through deliberate design of the employer or the personal choice of the labourer, its effect was to weaken the labourer's power to resist the institutions of credit which entangled him.

It may well be asked why labouring men did not perceive the plight they were in as clearly as their middle class critics. The answer is of course that some of them were fully aware of the way in which their partiality for drink was used to exploit them; and as a result a small, determined minority took the drastic step of becoming teetotallers. But the majority found it impossible to step outside the bounds of the culture in which they had been reared. Drinking was not a sort of optional extra, a personal taste which was the result of conscious choice. Rather, the system of rule and regulation as to times and occasions of drinking, pervades all branches of society in Great Britain – at meals, markets, fairs, baptisms, and funerals; and almost every trade and profession has its own code of strict and well-observed laws on this subject. There are numerous occasions when general custom makes the offer and reception of liquor as imperative as the law of the land.[12]

Drinking usages were woven into the very fabric of working class life. During working hours a wide variety of customs was enforced to extract payments for drink. Among skilled artisans footings, or payments on entry to the trade, were practically universal. The plumbers extracted money for drink when the apprentice cast his first sheet of lead, the blockcutters when he cut his first printing-block. In woollen mills the changing from one loom to another, the first lighting of the factory in the autumn, or the first time a young man was seen by his mates with a young woman (the 'bull shilling') were all made occasion for drink money. At fairs and markets bargains were sealed with a drink; and at North country hirings agricultural labourers were hired for the year amid a week-long celebration of drinking and inebriation. Trade unions and friendly societies usually met in public houses, the landlord providing a free room on the understanding that the members would buy drink.

For a labouring man to eschew drink in these circumstances was more than giving up a single habit: it was a repudiation of important aspects of working class community life. Conversely, adherence to drinking habits could be an assertion of independence, a resistance to the pressures for conformity to the values of the new industrial civilisation. Middle class temperance reformers were fully alive to the desirability of destroying relics of the old popular culture to which the northern and midland workers clung tenaciously. Traditional customs were condemned as 'the pastimes of village buffoonery and rudeness', and drinking habits were particularly deplored as hindering the establishment of new norms of work and social conduct. At this point we are back to the problem of the transformation of the labouring poor into the working classes.

In no respect was this transition more painful than in the changes to which the labouring family was subjected. It is a sad comment on British historiography that while we have a great many studies of political parties, trade unions and religious bodies, there is not a single history of the basic social institution of British life, the family. Until some attempt has been made to fill this gap it is impossible to write with assurance about family life in the nineteenth century, or to do more than hazard a few guesses at the nature of the impact of industrialism upon the home. That the family as an institution was subjected to very considerable pressures, and that as a result it began to change, seems highly likely in view of the concern expressed by contemporaries in the 1830s. But what the exact nature of this change was is very hard to judge. By the very nature of the case, information about such a private, even intimate institution as the family is difficult to obtain. Very few records of the internal life of a family, especially a working class family were ever kept. So that we have to rely on the observations of middle class investigators and novelists or the incidental remarks in the autobiographies of working men. On many important facets of the labouring family, such as the relations between parents and children, the regulation of sexual *mores*, or the authoritarian role of the father there is very little hard data. Something may in due course be gleaned from a closer examination of oral and folk tradition and by reworking primary sources that have already been used for other purposes. In the meantime we have always to be aware that some of what we 'know' about labouring families may in fact be a projection of contemporary middle class or modern ideals and assumptions.

Victorian comment on changes in the working class family was usually adverse: the effects of women going out to work, sexual irregularities outside the home, the downgrading of the role of the father. This state of affairs was contrasted with the domestic system and its stable family relationships which, it was alleged, were being destroyed. The critique was of course strongest for the factory districts or for any industry where the basis of organisation was shifting away from the home. In all such cases the economic role of the family changed, bringing with it consequent social dislocations and adjustments. As textiles set the pace of economic change, the strains and tensions within the family structure were felt earliest and most acutely in the manufacturing areas, though they were not confined to that part of the population.

Briefly, the charge was made that the factory system broke up the working class family. This it did in a number of ways. First, it physically separated the members of a family for 12 to 14 hours a day when some or all of them went off to work in the mill early in the morning and returned at night. The family as a unit was together only for purposes of sleeping, eating, and (on Sundays and holidays) recreation, whereas under the domestic system the members had been together at work and leisure all day and every day. Second, when a married woman went out to work her efficiency as a wife and mother was greatly reduced. She did not have time to do the housework, sewing and cooking except in the evenings, when she was tired, and on Sundays (when she should have been at church). The children were neglected because she was not at home to look after them. Third, unmarried girls who worked in the factories had no time to develop housewifely skills and were also encouraged in sexual immorality by the conditions of mill life. It was also stated that the factory system diminished respect for chastity in marriage and thereby undermined the family. Fourth, the strength of the married man's position in the family was weakened. When his wife and children were also bread-winners, and when he was separated from them all day his patriarchal authority was reduced. He was not able, as in domestic industry, to exercise the necessary control over his children, to train them daily in good habits and to exert an unchallenged leadership. Indeed, at times he might even be unemployed and at home, while his wife and daughters had to get work to support him.

The causes which have led to the present declension in the social and physical condition of the operatives ... have been wholly misunderstood [argued Dr Peter Gaskell]. It is not poverty ...; no, it has arisen from the separation of families, the breaking up of households.[13]

Gaskell, and others like him in the 1830s, were convinced that there had been a loss in the social and domestic happiness of labouring families, and regretted the disintegration of 'domestic virtues'. Cobbett had been saying the same thing for years; and Richard Oastler, 'the Factory King', thundered that the violation of the sacred nature of the home was the greatest curse of the factory system.

Without necessarily subscribing to the reformers' rather idyllic version of the domestic system, it is easy to appreciate certain genuine virtues in it which would have a strong appeal. Handloom weaving was an occupation for the whole family, and if the work was often monotonous and the hours long, the pace could be varied to suit individual needs, and the family was together for meals and rest periods. Relationships between members of the family and with neighbouring families could be established according to traditional values and a sense of what was just and right. Moreover, as Gaskell put it, 'The circumstances of a man's labour being conducted in the midst of his household exercised a powerful influence upon his social affections and those of his offspring'.[14] In general terms, the family was both a basic economic unit and the centre of a network of social relationships which had all the force of tradition behind them. Some aspects of this culture were crude, repressive and cruel, but in the main it provided a viable and stable way of life. Granted all of this, however, the question to be answered is, to what extent did this traditional family survive into the early Victorian period and how far was it replaced, whether through the demands of the factory system or other causes, by a new type of family?

With regard to the separation of the family during the day, every effort was made by the textile workers to resist this change. In the cotton industry they succeeded until the 1820s in maintaining something of the family relationship within the factory.[15] It was the custom for a skilled cotton spinner to hire his own assistants, usually two or three, and so he employed his wife and children or near relations. The family was thus kept together and the link between the economic and other functions of the family was preserved. In the 1820s, however, larger mules with more spindles were introduced which required anything from four to nine assistants. The spinner could not normally provide this number of helpers from among his own children and had to hire others, which diluted or undermined the family unit. At the same time changes in the weaving branch of the cotton industry also worked against the preservation of the family within the factory. Power looms were introduced widely in the late 1820s and early 1830s, and were operated by women and boys, not by fathers of families. The power loom weavers' assistants were appointed by the masters, not the operatives. No room was left for the employment of a family all together. This breakdown of the traditional family relationship within the factory accounts in part for the operatives' support of the factory movement in the 1830s. They agitated for a ten hour day for children, knowing that this would mean ultimately a ten hour day for adults as well. But the Factory Act of 1833 which emerged from these struggles limited children's labour to eight hours a day and made possible a relay system whereby the adults would continue to work long hours with the assistance of different shifts of child helpers. This did not suit the operatives' needs at all. It broke up the family unit in the mill and did not reduce adult hours. From 1833 therefore, the operatives demanded first an eight hour day for all, then a twelve hour day including the children, and finally settled for a universal ten hours, which meant actually extending the hours of children. Successive factory acts in 1844 and 1847 did not go back on the 1833 Act, but rather strengthened it by separating still further the hours and conditions of children from those of adults. In this way the earlier efforts to maintain family relationships in the factory were effectively ended.

The general conclusion would seem to be that by the 1830s and 1840s the families of weavers and spinners were not functioning economically or socially in the same way as they had done fifty years earlier. Attempts to prevent these changes were unsuccessful even by particularly well placed artisans like the cotton spinners. Other workers in the woollen industry and weavers in all branches of textiles had even less hope of maintaining traditional family roles. For workers who had not yet entered factories – handloom weavers, stockingers, nailmakers, cabinet-makers – the family retained more of its old character; though the low earnings and long hours stripped the family of many of its social values and left it little more than an effective instrument for economic oppression. Under such conditions the artisan's highly-prized independence was dearly bought.

If the trend in family change was towards a differentiation of the economic from other roles, the complexity of the issues which it raised is shown in the position of married women who went out to work. In the cotton districts in 1851, about 30 per cent of all married women were employed, and of these almost two-thirds were textile operatives. The percentage of married women who at some time had gone out to work would be higher than this. In Staffordshire the proportion of married women working in the potteries was about the same. To the factory reformers the problem was chiefly this: if a wife left home at six o'clock every morning and worked (with an hour's dinner break from 12.30 to 1.30) until six o'clock at night, how could she adequately look after the family? 'Where, sir,' asked Lord Ashley in 1844, 'under these conditions are the possibilities of domestic life?'[16] The most convenient solution of the wife's problems was to have a grand-mother or a young daughter not in the mill to look after the babies and do a little cooking and cleaning. Alternatively it was possible to hire a girl aged seven to eleven to do these chores for not more than 2s a week. There were also day nurses, usually old women, to whom babies could be taken during working hours. Children of working mothers had to be weaned early – in contrast to most working class children whose mothers breast-fed them as long as possible, hoping thereby to avoid another pregnancy. Infants in such homes did not, by modern standards, get very much or very careful attention, and Godfrey's cordial (a pacifier containing laudanum) was administered liberally.

To assess the gain or loss to the family of these developments is not an absolute matter but the striking of a balance. Probably the children were better off when their mother could interrupt her spinning or weaving to suckle them and when, as they grew bigger, they were subject to their father's training and correction. The married woman factory worker may have gained a new sense of independence in being away from the home and contributing to the family income; the unmarried girls certainly did. On the other hand the traditional measure of a woman's status was her skill in all the arts of home-craft, and by this conventional wisdom the factory girl, married or unmarried, was made to feel wanting. The removal of industry from the home to the factory was from the housewifely point of view a blessing. A home that was also a workshop could become very squalid. Not all handicraft industry was carried on in a specially built loomshop in a substantial stone house like the Yorkshire weaver's. The low-ceilinged living room of the Leicester stockinger was almost completely filled with his great clumsy wooden knitting frame, and the Black Country nailer's shed was a lean-to at the back of his cottage. Emancipation from the noise and dirt and smell of domestic industry must have been very welcome to those house-wives who remained at home – and these, after all, were more numerous than those who went out to work.

The trouble with this somewhat mechanical assessment of the situation is that the gains and losses were often intangible: feelings and emotions that were hard to measure, personal relationships that were not always easy to recognise. The family is the most conservative and stable of all our social institutions; it involves us deeply in the most fundamental aspects of human life. Changes in the family will therefore always be slow and usually painful. In the 1830s there was much alarmed talk about the break-up of the labouring family: the signs of change were apparent and were interpreted as yet more evidence of the seriousness of the condition-of-England question. From a social point of view what contemporaries were witnessing was a certain stage in the process of differentiation or specialisation of the family. Whereas previously the family had encompassed a number of different activities (economic, educational, recreational and sexual) now it was becoming more specialised. Other agencies and institutions were assuming some of its earlier functions.

One of the effects of differentiation was to bring the labouring family more into line with its middle class counterpart. In principle the middle classes could not but welcome such a development, but at the same time the disruption which the process of change involved made them apprehensive. Everywhere they feared the disruptive effects of 'immorality', and critics of the factory system expended some of their most fervid passion in denunciations of sexual irregularities in the mills. Against this danger, they claimed, stood the bastion of the family. How far the labouring family was in fact the regulator of sexual *mores*, and how far such an idea was wishful thinking by the middle classes is extremely difficult to determine. It is also difficult to ascertain whether sexual relationships of working people, either within or outside the family were changing. Gaskell thought that they were – and for the worse. He wrote of 'the almost entire extinction of sexual decency, which is one of the darkest stains upon the character of the manufacturing population – the laxity in all the moral obligations which ought to exist between the sexes'.[17] Girls who had been concubines, he averred, found no difficulty in marrying subsequently. He found among the factory population an 'entire absence of all regard for moral obligations relating to sex' extending to married and unmarried persons alike. A dominant theme of Gaskell's book, published in 1833 and re-issued in 1836, was the spread of sexual immorality and the decay of family virtue.

From what little is known of working class sexual relations it seems unwise to take Gaskell's strictures at their face value. The practices he deplored, and which he almost certainly exaggerated, were not peculiar to the factory operatives. Pre-marital sexual intercourse was common among labouring people, but was not usually promiscuous. It was rather an anticipation of the marriage bed by courting couples, and if pregnancy resulted marriage was arranged before the birth of the child. From agricultural areas there was plenty of evidence by vicars that most of the brides whom they married were pregnant on their wedding day. In his investigations of London street folk, Mayhew discovered various types of sexual relationship outside marriage. He esti-mated that only one-tenth of the costermonger couples who lived together were married. From the age of fifteen or sixteen a boy would set up as a trader with his own barrow and begin living with a girl of his own age, as man and wife. These were stable, lasting relationships and infidelity (at least by the girls) was disapproved of. 'If I seed my gal a talking to another chap I'd fetch her . . . a punch on the nose,' explained one young costermonger. And another lad opined that 'the gals – it was a rum thing now he come to think on it – axully liked a feller for walloping them. As long as the bruises hurted, she was always thinking on the cove as gived 'em her'.[18] This comforting masculine view, which suggests the possibility of a double standard of sexual morality among the working as well as the middle classes, would have been widely appreciated, if not openly approved in early Victorian society. Gaskell reserved his special horror for female unchastity, and laid upon the family the onus of controlling sexual relations. It is not clear, however, that this was one of the traditional roles of the labouring family; and, to the extent that it was not, it represented a new departure.

Problems of the labouring family, as with other aspects of the condition-of-England question, were encountered head-on in the enforcement of the Poor Laws. Superficially the Poor Laws were simply a matter of relief, but in fact they raised fundamental questions of social policy. The various aspects of the condition-of-England question were not for the most part regarded as appropriate for governmental action, but in the extreme case of destitution it had long been recognised that the state had an obligation to see that provision was made to relieve the distress. In a rural society, where the poor were taken for granted, the periodic need to help them beyond the extent of normal Christian charity was acknowledged. From Elizabethan times the responsibility for looking after its own poor was laid squarely upon each parish, under the direction of the justices of the peace. The Poor Law Act of 1601 provided overseers of the poor who were to levy a poor rate for the relief of the sick, aged and unemployed. With the spread of enclosures after 1760 and the rise in food prices during the French wars, the number of poor to be relieved increased rapidly, and the poor rates jumped accordingly. In 1775 they had amounted to less than £2 million, by 1801 they had doubled, and in 1831 they were nearly £7 million – provoking loud protestations from the rate-payers. In many districts the practice of granting outdoor relief to employed as well as unemployed labourers had grown up, and in 1795 this became semi-regularised as the 'Speenhamland system'. It was the intention of the justices at Speenhamland to help the poor by ensuring that each family had a minimum income calculated according to the price of bread and number of dependants, but the effect was to subsidise low wages out of poor rates. The system was adopted widely in the southern counties, and was held by orthodox political economists to be largely responsible for rural pauperisation. For over forty years the problem of how to reduce the growing burden of poor rates (which fell mainly on the farmers in the countryside and the middle classes in the towns) had been debated, without any conclusive result. But by the early 1830s the pressure to do away with the Old Poor Law and to create a free labour market in accordance with the principles of political economy was sufficiently strong to overcome working class radical and Tory opposition. In the autumn of 1830 the 'Swing' riots of agricultural labourers throughout the southern and eastern counties had been savagely put down (19 men hung, 644 imprisoned, 481 transported), and the new Whig government decided that drastic action was required. A Royal Commission on the Poor Laws was appointed, and its *Report* provided the basis for a New Poor Law, enacted in 1834.

The new law, like the old, accepted the principle that every necessitous person had a claim to relief; but the relief was to be given only under new and stricter conditions. First, out-door relief was to be abolished and all recipients made to enter the workhouse. Second, conditions in the workhouse were made 'less eligible' (i.e. more miserable) than the condition of the lowest paid worker outside. A rigorous workhouse test was thus applied to all applicants for relief, the intention being to deter all but the really 'deserving' (i.e. desperate) cases. To carry out this sweeping reform of the Old Poor Law system a centralised administration was established, consisting of a board of three commissioners, who in turn appointed regional assistant commissioners. The old parish workhouses were abolished and the parishes grouped together in 'unions', each with one large central workhouse. Boards of guardians were elected by the rate-payers in each Poor Law Union and were responsible for carrying out the regulations imposed by the commissioners.

The rationale of the New Poor Law lay in the doctrines of orthodox political economy. Anything which interfered with the working of the 'natural' laws of supply and demand was felt to be undesirable. By this test trade unions, factory regulations and poor relief stood alike condemned. The widespread acceptance among the educated classes of a *laissez-faire* philosophy, coupled with the desire to reduce the poor rates, ensured a sympathetic response to the Poor Law *Report* and support for the government's Act of 1834. Edwin Chadwick, the first secretary of the central board and drafter of the *Report*, was a disciple of Jeremy Bentham and an enthusiast for administrative reform. Nassau Senior, his colleague, was Professor of Political Economy at Oxford, and favoured doing away with the poor laws altogether. Between them they concocted a drastic revision of English social policy. Ramshackle and inefficient as the Old Poor Law had been, it nevertheless provided the rudiments of a system of social welfare: income maintenance for the poorest workers, unemployment compensation, and family endowment. This was now to be swept away, on the grounds that public charity was incompatible with the principles of the economists.

Critics, however, saw the matter differently. To Carlyle it was not the application of natural, scientific, or immutable laws of political economy but the application of a very simple and brutal axiom: 'If paupers are made miserable, paupers will needs decline in multitude. It is a secret known to all rat-catchers'.[19] And he sarcastically suggested that poisoning paupers, like rats, with arsenic would be even more efficient. The 'social principle' of the New Poor Law was no principle at all, he argued, but simply an attempt to sweep the problems of the poor and luckless out of sight. In one sense Carlyle was right: the New Poor Law was an attempt to deal not with the fundamental causes of destitution but only with its symptoms as expressed in the demand for relief. In other respects, however, the 1834 Act was a basic measure, for it defined the social policy of the state, as it affected a majority of the population, in a new way. The issue was more than the replacement of a lenient by a severe administration of the laws governing relief: it was the announcement that henceforth the labouring poor must abandon many of their traditional attitudes and expectations and conform to new standards of social and economic rectitude.

The new measures were greeted with bitter opposition from working people. Inevitably the poor laws affected the life of a labouring man at its most tender spots. In times of distress caused by unemployment, sickness, old age and death, the labouring man and his family were under strain, and most in need of sympathetic help and consideration. Yet this was the last thing to be expected under the new régime. As they watched the building of the great, grim new workhouses and heard the rumours of the prison-like discipline enforced behind the high walls, the working classes were seized with a great and sudden fear. On the outskirts of every medium-sized town and at remote cross roads in country districts the new, raw, red-brick buildings appeared. They looked like prisons and were christened the 'bastilles'. Inside them life was made as dreary and comfortless as was possible without actually endangering health. When a pauper family presented itself for relief at the gates of the workhouse it was immediately broken up, men, women and children being housed in separate parts of the building and forbidden to reunite as long as they remained. Able-bodied men were set to work at stone breaking, grinding corn or picking oakum. Food was plain and monotonous: mainly bread and gruel, with a small allowance of meat and cheese. Until 1842 all meals were eaten in silence, and smoking was forbidden. A special workhouse dress was worn, and the master of the workhouse was enjoined 'to enforce industry, order, punctuality and cleanliness' at all times. Visitors were allowed infrequently and only in the presence of the master or matron. The commissioners (and usually also the guardians) were specially keen that the greatest economy should be exercised, and any little comfort that might be considered a luxury was carefully excluded: an occasional cup of tea for the old folks or a few extra delicacies for Christmas dinner (even though paid for by a private benefactor) were considered exceedingly dubious relaxations of the regulations.

Such a system would have been sufficiently terrifying had all the masters and matrons, overseers and guardians been humane and honest. But given the normal incidence of sadism, greed and petty-mindedness among mankind, and the credulity with which reports of abuses are received, it was inevitable that the horror of the new workhouses would be magnified further. There were in any case sufficient bad cases to nourish the worst of contemporary fears and rumours: the two and a half year old child in Warwick workhouse who was punished for dirtying himself by having his own excrement forced into his mouth; the master of the Hoo Union workhouse who pruriently flogged teenage girls; the prisoner in Knutsford gaol who had been sent there for fetching his child into his own bed when he heard it crying during the night in another part of the workhouse in which he then was. Most notorious of all was the scandal in the Andover workhouse, where the paupers were so hungry that they fought among themselves for bits of gristle and marrow among the old bones they were set to crush. Typical of the insensitivity of the commissioners was the attempt in 1836 to save the cost of tolling the bell at pauper funerals. The desire for a respectable burial was (and long remained) deeply ingrained in the English poor, and Chadwick's circular was an outrage upon their feelings of common decency. The New Poor Law was by its very nature a piece of class legislation, in that decisions affecting one class (the poor) were made by another. Even so, it was unusually blatant in the way it trampled on so much that the labouring poor held dear.

In so far as the New Poor Law was an attempt to deal with pauperism rather than poverty, its results could be judged fairly satisfactory. Applied first to the southern counties, where rural pauperism was worst, and helped by two good harvests and the demand for labour to build railways, the abuses of the allowance (or Speenhamland) system were speedily removed, and the old evil of underemployment in agriculture largely disappeared. To this extent the New Poor Law succeeded in its aim of restoring the labourer to something like a condition of formal independence. The social disease of pauperism, it was argued, had been cured by the drastic but necessary surgery of cutting off out-door relief. In fact the guardians in rural areas had to continue out-door relief for the able-bodied in cases of urgency as well as for some of the aged and infirm. When the commissioners turned their attention to the industrial districts in 1837, they found even less possibility of a blanket application of the new regulations to all and sundry. The needs of industrial workers were not the same as for agricultural labourers, and moreover they were on the brink of the worst economic depression of the nineteenth century. Factory operatives and hand workers were not suffering the effects of an allowance system which artificially depressed wages; they required short-term relief to tide them over periods of temporary unemployment until good times returned. They regarded the idea of having to enter the workhouse in order to get relief as monstrous, and totally irrelevant to their real needs. The resistance to the New Poor Law in the northern towns delayed its introduction for many months, but by 1840 Poor Law Unions were established throughout the country. It proved impossible to implement all the principles of the 'harsh but salutary act': out-door relief simply could not be completely abolished, nor did the mixed workhouse (catering for all types of indigent poor from orphans to old people, able-bodied and sick), which had been condemned in the 1834 *Report*, disappear. The principle of less eligibility, however, was sufficiently enforced to make the workhouse a terror and shame to ordinary people. Its shadow fell across the lives of labouring men, reminding them always of the price of indigency.

The attack on out-relief owed much to the influence of Malthus, and the New Poor Law as a whole reflected accurately the dominant social philosophy of the middle classes. Carlyle interpreted the New Poor Law as 'an announcement, sufficiently distinct, that whosoever will not work ought not to live'.[20] To the problem of the man who was willing to work but for whom no work was available no satisfactory answer was forthcoming. It was an assumption of the New Poor Law that pauperism was in most cases culpable, that indigency was due largely to personal weakness. From this it followed that improvement could be effected by individual effort, given the necessary will and determination. The condition-of-England question was to be solved by the great Victorian panacea, self-help.

4

Patterns of Prosperity: The Middling and Upper Classes

It will be apparent from the preceding chapters that not very much of the great increase in national wealth had trickled through to the labouring poor. The basis for Porter's optimism about the Progress of the Nation was to be found mainly elsewhere, notably in the condition of that growing section of the community called the middling or middle classes, and the landowners. Between these prosperous groups and the army of the poor the contrast was very great. The age-old categorisation of society into the rich and the poor was as meaningful as ever. In their homes and habits and whole culture the affluent classes were, in many respects, as far removed from their poorer countrymen as if they had been inhabitants of a foreign land. William Howitt was struck by the great distance, in rural England, between the hall and the cottage:

What a mighty space lies between the palace and the cottage in this country! ay, what a mighty space between the mansion of the private gentleman and the hut of the labourer on his estate! To enter the one: to see its stateliness and extent; all its offices, out-buildings, gardens, greenhouses, hothouses; its extensive fruit-walls, and the people labouring to furnish the table simply with fruit, vegetables, and flowers; its coach-houses, harness-houses, stables, and all the steeds, draught-horses, and saddle-horses, hunters, and ladies' pads, ponies for ladies' airing-carriages, and ponies for children; and all the grooms and attendants thereon; to see the waters for fish, the woods for game, the elegant dairy for the supply of milk and cream, curds and butter, and the dairymaids and managers belonging to them; – and then, to enter the house itself and see all its different suites of apartments, drawing-rooms, boudoirs, sleeping-rooms, dining and breakfast rooms; its steward's, housekeeper's and butler's rooms; its ample kitchens and larders, with their stores of provisions, fresh and dried; its stores of costly plate, porcelain and crockery apparatus of a hundred kinds; its cellars of wine and strong beer; its stores of linen; its library of books, its collections of paintings, engravings, and statuary; the jewels, musical instruments, and expensive and interminable nick-knackery of the ladies; the guns and dogs; and cross-bows, long bows, nets, and other implements of amusement of the gentlemen; all the rich carpeting and fittings-up of day-rooms and night-rooms, with every contrivance and luxury which a most ingenious and luxurious age can furnish; and all the troops of servants, male and female, having their own exclusive offices, to wait upon the person of lady or gentleman, upon table, or carriage, or upon some one ministration of pleasure or necessity: I say, to see all this, and then to enter the cottage of a labourer, we must certainly think that one has too much for the insurance of comfort, or the other must have extremely too little . . .

When we go into the cottage of the working man, how forcibly are we struck with the difference between his mode of life and our own. There is his tenement of, at most, one or two rooms. His naked walls; bare brick, stone or mud floor, as it may be; a few wooden, or rush-bottomed chairs; a deal or old oak table; a simple fireplace, with its oven beside it, or, in many parts of the kingdom, no other fireplace than the hearth; a few pots and pans – and you have his whole abode, goods and chattels. He comes home weary from his out-door work, having eaten his dinner under hedge or tree, and seats himself for a few hours with his wife and children, then turns into a rude bed, standing perhaps on the farther side of his only room, and out again before daylight, if it be winter. . . .[1]

The pattern of prosperity outlined here belonged to the most ancient and prestigious group among the wealthy, the owners of land. From time immemorial land had been regarded as a very special form of property: the lawyers distinguished it as 'real' property. It was felt to be the most permanent of all forms of wealth; it was the foundation of the most basic of human activities, the production of food; and it was inherited from generation to generation. Landed property conferred a stability and continuity greater than any other material possessions, and provided institutions and forms of authority which have lasted from feudal times to the present day. To possess a landed estate has been (and still is) the ambition of generations of 'successful' Englishmen: it was the surest way to recognition as a gentleman. The strength of the mystique of landed property is attested by the extent to which a social order based on land not only survived but flourished in an increasingly industrial world. Throughout the nineteenth century landed society retained its position of superiority and leadership. It survived three reform bills and the onset of first middle class and then mass democracy. Long after the relative decline of agriculture and the transition to an industrial state, the tone of British society in its upper echelons was still set by the great houses and the owners of broad acres. Yet landed England did not survive unchanged. Had there not been a flexibility in coming to terms with the economic realities of the industry state, and a willingness to retreat gradually and quietly from untenable positions of political privilege, landed society might not have outlived the end of the century. In fact it displayed remarkable powers of tenacity and adaptation: it sought to engulf and change some of the new elements in society, though in the process it was itself changed.

In early Victorian Britain the landed interest embraced everyone who was in some way connected with agriculture, including tenant farmers and wage labourers as well as landowners. An economic basis for this was found in an assumed identity of interest in the fortunes of the farming industry. Socially, rural England was held together by the bonds of deference; that is to say, the lower orders habitually deferred to their 'betters' and accorded them the respect due to rank and title. Within the ranks of landowners the lesser normally deferred to the greater. Deference was for the most part voluntary in the sense that it was the automatic acceptance by the majority of the claims and assumptions of an élite as being part of the natural order of things (though it would be naïve to overlook the economic dependence of tenant farmers, agricultural labourers and servants on their own particular landlord or employer). The tremendous self-confidence and authoritarian style of the upper classes, their easy assumption of an inborn right and duty to lead others, and their superior education and (frequently) physical endowments set them apart from other men. Their claim to hereditary authority was seldom questioned by those who had grown up in the shadow of the hall or great house, and the urban middle classes as a body were content to defer to them in many areas of national life. Small wonder that Walter Bagehot in his famous book on *The English Constitution* (1867) could describe England as the very type of a deferential country.

The landowners who provided this traditional leadership fell into two groups, the aristocracy and the gentry.[2] At the top of the landed hierarchy was a small group of about three hundred families who owned large estates and enjoyed an income of at least £10,000 a year. Some had as much as £50,000 a year; others fell below £10,000 but compensated for this by possession of a peerage or unusually ancient lineage. The members of this landed aristocracy were known by their titles: dukes, marquises, earls, viscounts and barons; and the heads of these families formed the peerage and sat in the House of Lords. Normally a member of the aristocracy could be expected to have an estate of at least 10,000 acres, with a mansion in the country and a town house in London, between which he divided his time. By intermarriage the aristocracy was a closely-knit group, based on a series of alliances between independent families, whose name and reputation were a source of jealous pride.

Life amongst the aristocracy was on the grand scale. A great house in the country was a complete community, which generated its own social and economic life and made its influence felt in the county for many miles around. In addition to the members of the family and their guests, a staff of forty or fifty servants was to be expected, and the footmen and coachmen were in livery. Nothing less than a small palace was adequate to house such numbers, and great areas of the countryside were reserved as parks for the exclusive enjoyment of noblemen and their friends. As with royalty, the normal events of life became public occasions. The birth of an heir, the marriage of children and the death of the head of a family were observed with due ceremony by the local villagers and lesser gentry. In 1845, when the Marquis of Worcester, son and heir of the Duke of Beaufort came of age, two hundred tenants were feasted in the servants' hall at Badminton, an ox was roasted, and the celebrations were continued for a week. Some of the nobility possessed several country houses, and so spent the year in different parts of the country: an estate in Yorkshire was convenient for the grouse shooting season, one in the milder southern counties was preferable for the winter, and a luxurious town house in the West End was essential for the London season. An almost continual round of hospitality was observed in the great houses, with sport of various kinds providing the main entertainment. The actual management of the estates was delegated to stewards and bailiffs, leaving the nobleman himself free to devote his time to county and national affairs. In a deferential society aristocratic leadership, while it preserved the interests of a privileged minority, also provided a form of public service.

At the local level this leadership and service was undertaken by the lesser landowners, the country gentry. Their estates were anything from 1,000 to 10,000 acres, with corresponding incomes of £1,000 to £10,000 a year. There were perhaps three thousand landed gentry, of whom two thousand were village squires living on estates of 1,000 to 3,000 acres. Some of the gentry were knights and baronets (a sort of hereditary knighthood) but the majority had no title beyond that of gentlemen. Unlike the aristocracy they normally could not afford a town house, and so lived on their estates the year round, occupying themselves with village and county matters. Typically, the squire lived in his hall or manor house, surrounded by a small garden and home farm managed by a bailiff. The rest of his land was subdivided into farms which were let to tenant farmers, whose rents provided the main income of the estate. As with the aristocracy, the estate was preserved intact from generation to generation by the custom of the eldest son or daughter inheriting it all, instead of subdividing the inheritance among the younger children.

Ever since Elizabethan times the gentry, through the institution of the justice of the peace, had provided the crucial element in the government of rural England. Sitting on the local bench they dispensed rough and ready justice to their tenants and villagers. At the quarter sessions in the local county town they tried more serious cases and dealt with administrative chores. At the Brewster Sessions they supervised the licensing of public houses. They saw to the operation of the Poor Laws through the local board of guardians; they officered the local yeomanry (volunteer cavalry troops); and they and their wives promoted charitable efforts among the poor. None of these duties was pursued to the point where it might become burdensome. A landed gentleman's life was essentially a life of leisure: unlike the labouring man or the merchant or industrialist, whose preoccupation was making a living, the country gentleman enjoyed an inherited income and spent his time doing the things that pleased him. Since comparatively few of the gentry had any intellectual or sustained political interests, their lives fell into a routine of social entertainments and obligations. They visited and dined regularly with neighbouring families, they enjoyed a round of balls and social occasions when they met together in the county town for the quarter sessions, and they indulged their taste for field sports to the full.

To William Howitt it seemed that the English country gentleman was in the most enviable position 'as regards all the pleasures and advantages of life'. Coming down in the morning he would find on his breakfast-table the London papers of the previous evening, bringing him the latest news from all parts of the globe. Amidst the peace and quiet of his woods and groves he enjoyed a meal containing delicacies equal to anything in the metropolis. When breakfast was over he was free to choose what he should do that day: whether to spend his time in his library or among his paintings and works of art, or outside in his garden and park and farm. For the ladies there were

books, music, the garden, the conservatory – an abundance of elegant and womanly occupations. There are drives through woods and fields of the most delicious character; there is social intercourse with neighbouring wealthy families, and a host of kind offices to poor ones, which present the sweetest sources of enjoyment.[3]

The reality usually fell short of Howitt's idyllic description. Perhaps nearer the mark is a letter from a young American girl, Anna Maria Fay, who was visiting her uncle on an estate at Moor Park, Shropshire, in 1851:

> We rise early at half-past seven, have prayers at half-past eight, and breakfast a quarter of an hour later. After breakfast the children go to their schoolroom and Maria gives Kitty a music lesson. Aunt Catherine and I write or sew until eleven or twelve, when we go out driving. Uncle Richard either goes shooting by himself or with Mr Betton, and sometimes with Sir Charles Cuyler. We lunch when we return, and at six we dine. In the evening we form a very cheerful party by the drawing-room fire, reading, or sewing, or playing games with the children.[4]

Anna Fay soon discovered the intense devotion of the aristocracy and gentry to field sports: racing, hunting, coursing, shooting, fishing. For many of them sport became the central activity in life, to which other pursuits and duties were subordinated. The breeding and preservation of game was a highly organised industry, under the supervision of full-time gamekeepers, of whom there were about three thousand in Great Britain. They carried on a never-ending war with poachers, who if caught could hope for little mercy from the landowner-magistrate before whom they were brought for trial. Spring-guns (designed to fire automatically when the hidden trigger mechanism was set off by a trespasser) were only outlawed in 1827; and even though the penalties for poaching were modified in 1828, transportation was still the punishment for a third offence or if carrying a weapon with other poachers. Between 1827 and 1830, 1,500 persons were convicted under the Game Laws – one-seventh of all criminal convictions. Shooting parties lasting several days were popular among the aristocracy, and at these *battues* hundreds, sometimes thousands, of birds were slaughtered. The gentry, on a more modest scale, invited each other for a day's shooting, or simply spent several afternoons a week out with a dog and gun. In the evenings they relived their experiences during the day, as Anna Fay observed at a dinner party to which she was invited:

On my right hand I had Mr Landon, who is deaf in his left ear; and on my left, Mr Charlton, who informed me that he was deaf in his right ear. Notwithstanding the prospect thus opened, I had a very pleasant time. They were all sociable and agreeable. ... Then that never-ending theme of poachers came up. I cannot imagine what English country gentlemen would do were there no poachers. Mention the word, and you set Mr Betton off. He fights all his battles o'er again. He enlarges upon the villainy of poachers, upon the ingratitude of poachers, tells anecdotes about poachers, until you grow so nervous that you expect to see a poacher start up and seize the bird upon your plate. Naturally the conversation turns upon the day's sport, and you hear how that bird was winged: how another was tailered: how many cock pheasants were shot: how many hen pheasants were deprived of life: how many woodcock were put up; how many partridges flew out of one cover; how many rabbits were killed; who shot well; who shot badly; who missed fire; whose cock pheasant fell with his tail up; whose hen pheasant with her tail down; who shot on this side the dingle, who on the other, and so forth, and so forth, and so on. Then the meet of the previous day takes its turn – who fell in leaping over this hurdle, who in taking that hedge, who fell on his feet, who on his head, where the fox was found, and where killed, and how the sport was spoiled on account of the frost, and how cold it was, and how cold it is, and how cold it is going to be, and how unusual it is, such weather unheard of át this season, and how fine the autumn has been – and then you rise from the table and you leave the gentlemen to discuss, more at large, poaching, shooting, hunting, and the cold, unrestrained by female society. After a while they come into the drawing-room and the card-table is taken out, the gentleman cut to play and the rest look on. They are not a very intellectual set, these country gentlemen, but they are very sociable and pleasant.[5]

The great passion of the landed gentry was foxhunting, which by the 1840s had become an elaborate, ritualistic and exclusive cult. A territorial division of the counties allocated to each hunt its own area, and the expense and organisation devolved upon the local devotees of the chase. In some areas a member of the aristocracy undertook the leadership and finance of the hunt, but more often it was based upon the subscriptions of the local gentry. In either case the expense was considerable. The feeding, kennelling, breeding and exercising of the pack of foxhounds was the first charge; the hunt servants (whippers-in, huntsmen, kennel boys) had to be paid, boarded, and their livery provided; special coverts for the foxes had to be maintained, and gates and bridges provided at strategic points in the hunt's country. In addition, each foxhunter had to provide his own horses and equipment. At the head of the establishment was the Master of Fox Hounds (MFH) – perhaps the most coveted and respected position in county society. Foxhunting was not regarded as an amusing hobby, to be indulged in by interested individuals; rather was it felt to be a peculiarly national institution, deeply rooted in the finest and manliest elements of Old England. It was essentially a concern of the whole rural community, whose tacit cooperation was essential for the successful prosecution of the sport. Prosperous farmers, parsons and professional men rode to hounds – happy to be able to associate, even if only remotely, with the squire and his friends, and to receive a nod of recognition from a much-admired MFH. As a social institution foxhunting was an effective assertion of gentlemanly leadership and the bonds of deference.

The mystique of foxhunting was fed by the almost legendary exploits of a handful of sporting landowners. Thomas Assheton Smith, the squire of Tedworth, Hampshire, literally spent his life in the saddle: he hunted for seventy years and was MFH for nearly fifty. In 1856, in his eightieth year, he still hunted four days a week, while regretting he could not do more. If he felt himself not quite well in a morning he used to plunge his head into cold water and hold it there as long as he could. This, he said, always put him to rights. As Tory MP for Andover (1821–31) and Caernarvonshire (1832–41), it was his practice to hunt his hounds at Tedworth in the morning, then post in his light carriage with four horses to Westminster by the evening, and, after voting in the division, be back at Tedworth for a noon meet the next day. As a cricketer and pugilist he displayed great prowess, but his overriding passion was foxhunting. Other sports were but a means of filling in the summer months, while the hounds were idle. 'At the fall of the leaf,' records his devoted biographer, 'he was promptly in the saddle again.'[6] Nimrod, the popular sporting journalist, described Assheton Smith as the best and hardest rider England ever saw, and the Duke of Wellington referred to him as the Field Marshal of Foxhunting.

Even more prodigious physical feats were performed by George Osbaldeston (1787–1866), a Yorkshire squire who was a MFH while an undergraduate at Oxford. He killed a hundred pheasants with a hundred shots, could hit the ace of diamonds ten times out of ten with a pistol at thirty feet, and rode two hundred miles in ten consecutive hours. His courage, recklessness and physical toughness were highly regarded in an age which was tolerant of eccentricity and took a certain pride in its 'characters' among the gentry and aristocracy. In Regency times these qualities had been cultivated almost for their own sake. By the early Victorian period they were valued as desirable, manly foibles in a character otherwise distinguishable by kindness and public service. As a stereotype for the obituary of a foxhunting squire the following description of Assheton Smith could hardly be bettered:

His character – personal appearance and habits – impetuosity of temper – generosity of disposition – skill in games and sports – kindness to animals and liberality to his servants – his strong sense of justice – high character as a Master of Hounds, and as a daring horseman – testimony of his contemporaries.[7]

Assheton Smith's sporting life was not supported entirely out of his landed estate in Hampshire. Tucked away in his *Reminiscences* are references to his slate quarries in North Wales, from which he derived a handsome income. This was not untypical. In a variety of ways landed society tapped the new wealth of industry, trade and banking. There was nothing new in this: the alliance between old and new wealth had been going on since Elizabethan times, and there was an old saying that 'gentry is but ancient riches'. In early Victorian Britain it was the context of the alliance that was new. For the first time the balance of economic and political power had shifted in favour of industry and commerce, and the landed interest felt threatened. The symbol of this conflict was the repeal of the Corn Laws in 1846 – usually presented as the outcome of a struggle between the advocates of agricultural protection (the Corn Laws put a tariff on imported corn) and the industrialists who wanted cheap bread for their workers. The landed gentry (unlike some of the aristocracy, who were more Whiggish and less parochial in their outlook) bitterly opposed repeal and prognosticated the ruin of English agriculture and a drastic fall in their rents. They need not have worried: British agriculture flourished as never before until the 1870s. Nor need they have feared ruin from the effects of the 1832 Reform Bill. Despite the enfranchisement of the middle classes and the abolition of the old corrupt boroughs, a majority of the House of Commons came from landed families until well after 1867. The middle classes did not aim to destroy the landed interest; they undermined its power while deferring to its political and social leadership. Although middle class radicals of the Manchester School talked of the need to attack the institutions of aristocratic power, successful industrialists and merchants usually preferred to join the landed gentry if they could. The process was assimilation and was mutually advantageous. To the squirearchy it brought access to some of the wealth of the new industrialism; to the middle classes it brought the exclusive social prestige which only land could bestow.

There were several ways in which the process of assimilation was effected. Primogeniture forced the younger sons of the gentry to look elsewhere than the land for their livelihood, and so they entered business and the professions. Again, contact with the world of industry and finance could come through the discovery and exploitation of minerals, especially coal, on an estate; or through the windfall of urban site values near an expanding town. Marriage was the traditional, and probably still the most effective, form of alliance with new wealth, and provided for the middle classes a way of entry into landed society. Purchase of a landed estate was not too difficult for a successful merchant or industrialist, and provided he scrupulously followed the conventions of the county he could reasonably hope to be accepted by the local gentry in due course. If not, his children and grandchildren would normally be able to overcome the stigma of non-gentle birth.

The cotton spinner or brewer who bought the estate might never be fully accepted as a squire; his children would be brought up and go to school with members of the landed classes, but would retain some interest in the business; their children would be completely assimilated to the landed gentry and know little or nothing of the original business. Such was the pattern with many of the pioneer families of the Industrial Revolution: the Marshalls of Leeds, the Peels of Tamworth, the Strutts of Belper. To be acknowledged as a brave rider to hounds, to become a justice of the peace, and to intermarry one's children with the local gentry were the ambitions of the newcomers. Success in these endeavours was the outward sign of acceptance as a member of the landed interest. Assimilation of the new wealth on these terms meant abandoning middle class habits and modes, and adopting the culture of the landed gentry. Thus, while the middle class was ultimately the agency by which the power of pre-industrial, landed society was undermined, the middle class also retained and adapted the forms of gentility as means to preserve social leadership and deference.

At the aristocratic level alliance with new wealth was equally desirable. There were always impecunious noblemen looking for heiresses to retrieve the family fortunes, though they were not always successful since there were not enough wealthy bankers' daughters to go round. Lord Henry Thynne, a younger son of the Marquess of Bath was lucky. In 1830 he married the daughter of Alexander Baring, a rich banker who accumulated an estate in Hampshire and was later created Baron Ashburton. The daughter brought a marriage portion of £50,000, to be matched by Lord Henry's £10,000. Coal and railways brought fortunes to landowners as lucky as the Duke of Northumberland and Earl Fitzwilliam. The expansion of London was even more lucrative in the rents it created for the Portland, Grosvenor, Sidmouth and Russell families. Investment in docks, harbours and real estate in rapidly-growing industrial towns, also ensured that the aristocracy shared in the prosperity created by the new middle classes. Thus although landed wealth declined relative to other forms of wealth in the nation at large, the aristocracy was able to maintain a high level of material prosperity and to assert its traditional role of a ruling élite throughout most of the nineteenth century.

Between the nobility and the squirearchy there could be wide differences in wealth and social prestige, but they were basically a homogeneous group of highly privileged landowners. They were 'the gentlemen of England'. When anyone in early Victorian times was asked to define exactly what he meant by gentleman he had as much difficulty as we do today. Anthony Trollope, the novelist, who spent the 1840s in Ireland as a Post Office surveyor because he could lead the life of a foxhunting gentleman more cheaply there than in England, confessed in his posthumous *Autobiography* that although a man might be defied to define the term gentleman, everyone knew what he meant. Essentially the term was held to include gentle birth, ownership of a landed estate, and an income sufficient to permit the enjoyment of leisure. But the concept of gentility also implied certain moral qualities – honour, courage, consideration for others – which were embodied in a fairly strict code of what was 'done' and 'not done'. An affront to a gentleman's 'honour', for example, could be expiated only by a duel – a practice which continued into the 1850s. What was most clearly expected of a gentleman was public service, given voluntarily and if necessary at his own expense. In return he was accorded immense respect and his authority and privileges were accepted. The concept of gentility functioned as an agency of social discipline. Moreover, in a deferential society some of the attributes of gentility rubbed off on those lower down the social scale. Every foreign visitor knew that Englishmen loved to ape their betters ('How the English love a lord'); and the Victorian middle classes were no exception in their anxiety to rise socially.

The difference between a would-be gentleman and the genuine article is amusingly depicted in R.S.Surtees' novel, *Handley Cross*, published in 1843. Mr John Jorrocks, a prosperous Cockney grocer, develops an enthusiasm for hunting and the life of a country gentleman. He rides to hounds with a local Surrey pack, and then one day receives an invitation from an impecunious hunt to become their MFH. His joy knows no bounds, and

he composes a reply to Captain Doleful, the secretary of the
Handley Cross foxhounds:

> I am a sportsman all over, and to the back-bone. – 'Unting is all that's
> worth living for – all time is lost wot is not spent in 'unting – it is like
> the hair we breathe – if we have it not we die – it's the sport of kings,
> the image of war without its guilt, and only five-and-twenty per cent
> of its danger.

He has no doubt but that he is fully qualified for the mastership,
but his tradesman's shrewdness soon pops out: 'enough of the
rhapsodies, let us come to the melodies – the L.s.d. in fact. Wot will
it cost? – In course it's a subscription pack – then say how many
paying subscribers have you?' The humour of the novel comes
from the social incongruity of Jorrocks' vulgar, good-natured,
commonsensical outlook and the superior airs and pretensions of
the local pseudo-gentry. Jorrocks is not a snob, and in fact is
proud of his middle class status:

> Folks talk about the different grades o' society, but arter all's said
> and done there are but two sorts o' folks i' the world, Peerage folks and
> Post Hoffice Directory folks – Peerage folks, wot think it's all right
> and proper to do their tailors, and Post Hoffice Directory folks wot
> think it's the greatest sin under the sun not to pay twenty shillins i' the
> pund.

Significantly, *Handley Cross* was not a success when it was first
published. It was only later in the century that Jorrocks and his
bons mots ('Come hup, I say, you hugly beast') became household
words. In the 1840s foxhunting was at the height of its social
preeminence, and the MFH an almost sacred office to devotees.
Had Jorrocks been a completely ridiculous figure, Surtees'
sporting readers would have approved; but they were uneasy
when they realised they were expected to laugh not always at,
but sometimes with Jorrocks. They were not yet ready to accept
the homely, tradesman's philosophy of the middle classes at its
face value. In the 1830s and 1840s the structure of deference seemed
threatened by the great controversies over the Reform Bill and
the Corn Laws; surely, it was felt, these were not the times to
weaken further the public image of the institutions of deference.

During the next twenty years, when it became apparent that the stability of society had not been upset, it was possible to view Jorrocks more leniently. Moreover, he had gained a new readership, one more likely to appreciate, because it could identify with his special qualities – the middle classes.

Early Victorians talked a lot about the middle classes. Whether one approved or disapproved of them, the middle classes attracted attention for they seemed to be a more important section of the community than they had ever been before. Karl Marx and Friedrich Engels in the *Communist Manifesto* (1848) condemned the bourgeoisie (as they called the wealthy middle class) for the crime of 'shameless, direct, brutal exploitation' of everyone and everything. G.R.Porter and Richard Cobden (the Anti-Corn Law Leaguer) praised the middle classes as the standard-bearers of all that was most advanced and noble in contemporary civilisation. Historians too have divided over the issue of whether to blame the middle classes for accumulating wealth at the price of social misery for others, or praise them for creating a society with the potentiality of more freedom and abundance for all. Today we have some difficulty in defining the middle class, perhaps because many more people than formerly imagine they are members of it. In early Victorian England the tests of membership were more objective, though not by any means rigid or even definite. An income above a certain minimum was the first requisite. A particular occupation or calling was also useful in identifying a person as middle class. Education, religious affiliation and style of home provided further distinguishing characteristics. Even so, within these limits wide differences in wealth and status were possible, and it is therefore convenient to distinguish between *the haute bourgeoisie* and the lower middle class. The very top level of the middle classes lived on terms of familiarity with the aristocracy and, as we have seen, intermarried with them. London bankers and City merchants were some of the wealthiest people in the country, and together with their provincial counterparts formed a small financial oligarchy. The industrial magnates dominated the regional scene: coal and iron masters in South Wales, mill owners in Yorkshire and Lancashire, engineers and shipbuilders in Liverpool and Scotland. By the early Victorian period these men of business and industry had founded dynasties. The firm was now in the hands of the founder's sons or grandsons, who were no longer parvenus but members of a recognised provincial élite. This was a hierarchical but not a closed group, open ultimately to anyone who could become wealthy and gain respect.

In the 1830s and 1840s there were new opportunities for acquiring wealth, especially through the business of railroading. Two contrasting examples will show the possibilities and temptations that were open to middle class talent. Thomas Brassey was articled to a land surveyor, and through the encouragement of George Stephenson began contracting for railway construction in 1834. By 1845 he had on his hands thirteen large contracts for about 800 miles of railway in various parts of Great Britain and France. He extended his operations on a global scale, building railways in all parts of Europe as well as in India, South America, Canada, Australia and Mauritius. At his death in 1870 he left a fortune of several million pounds, despite financial difficulties in the crisis of 1866. He laid out £78 million of other people's money in railways, from which his overall return was about 3 per cent. At peak periods in his career he and his partners were giving employment to 80,000 persons upon works involving an investment of £17 million of capital. Brassey was a gentle-natured man who hated contention and who lived modestly, with few interests beyond his all-absorbing work.

Very different in temperament and fortune was George Hudson, 'the Railway King'. He was not a builder of railways but a promoter of railway companies. Son of a Yorkshire farmer, he became a linen draper in York, and with the help of some inherited property launched out into the new field of railroading. In 1833 he was treasurer of a committee to promote a line from Leeds to Selby, and three years later was chairman of a line linking York, Leeds and London. He then became manager of the York and North Midland Railway Company, opened in 1839, of the Newcastle and Darlington, 1842, and of the newly-formed Midland Railway in 1843-4. This was only a start: he went on to acquire holdings in other railway companies, in banking and in a dock company. In his home town of York he was twice made Lord Mayor (1837 and 1846), for his policy of amalgamation ('Mak all t'railways cum t'York') was understandably popular. By 1845 he was a millionaire, and in that year became MP for Sunderland. His success in gambling in railway stock made him a national figure, and in London he was lionised by high society and befriended by Prince Albert. A public testimonial for him raised £30,000 in three months and enabled him to buy and furnish Albert House, near Hyde Park. Another £25,000 was subscribed for a statue to this stocky, blunt, broad-spoken Yorkshireman, or, as Carlyle preferred to put it, 'offered as an oblation, by the Hero-worshippers of England to their Ideal of a Man'. Unfortunately for his worshippers Hudson's prosperity was not soundly based. In the summer of 1849 his dishonest practices were exposed: it was discovered that he had paid dividends out of capital and had been guilty of other financial irregularities. Nearly £80 million was lost by investors. Swiftly his empire collapsed, his creditors pressed hard, and only his membership of Parliament saved him from imprisonment for debt. He resigned the chairmanships of his numerous railway companies, and in 1854 retired to the Continent. Hudson Street in York had its name changed to Railway Street.

Tycoons like George Hudson were not representative of a majority of the middle classes – though they did highlight some of the implications of general middle class attitudes and assumptions. The majority, whom we have designated the lower middle class, were much more prosaic. As Bagehot wrote a little later, the £10 householders were people 'who have nothing imposing about them, nothing which would attract the eye or fascinate the fancy'. They were small manufacturers, shopkeepers, coal and corn merchants, master tailors, inn keepers, commercial travellers, dealers of all kinds – in a word, 'tradesmen'. To them should be added a growing army of clerks, office workers, schoolteachers and the lower ranks of the professions. Officials in government service and on the railways, managers in large industrial concerns, and qualified engineers also have to be included. By aristocratic criteria the lower middle classes were distinguished by the taint of trade or the performance of some paid service; by their own criteria they were respectable people who did not have to live by their manual labour.

The concept of a middle class standard of living was clearly developed by the 1830s.[8] It provided objectively a set of standards by which membership of the middle class could be determined, and subjectively a set of goals and minimum expectations to be striven for. The middle classes of early Victorian Britain were aware of themselves to a greater degree than in the past. Discontent with some aspects of aristocratic society on the one hand, and concern for working class poverty on the other, heightened this middle class selfconsciousness. As the middle classes opposed aristocratic idleness and excess with their puritan values of hard work and sobriety, or held themselves up as a model to the labouring poor and preached to them the doctrines of Malthus, they constantly reminded themselves of their distinctive position. The middle classes (perhaps more than the working classes) were class conscious. Determinants of social class in Britain have always been complex, if not downright confusing, but in the case of the early Victorian middle classes we have the guidance of contemporary writers who refer time and again to the same criteria: income and occupation, types of expenditure, and pattern of family living.

Basic to all middle class life was an income of at least a certain minimum. Moreover this income had to be steady and (desirably) progressive, and derived from a non-manual job in business or the professions. The figure of £300 a year was frequently mentioned as a minimum necessary for the normal range of middle class expectations, but people with tastes for greater comfort could easily consume twice or three times that sum. On the other hand a majority of the lower middle classes earned only £150 or £200 a year, and clerks and teachers as little as £60 – less than a skilled artisan. Anthony Trollope started as a clerk in the General Post Office in 1834 at a salary of £90 per annum, which after seven years' service had risen to £140. He regarded this as totally inadequate for even a tolerably comfortable life in

London, and was barely satisfied with the £400 a year which he was making in Ireland when he married in 1844. Only after a promotion to surveyor at £800, together with an income from his novels of £600 a year, did he feel satisfied: 'I was still living in Ireland, and could keep a good house over my head, insure my life, educate my two boys, and hunt perhaps twice a week, on £1,400 a year. ... It had been slow in coming, but was very pleasant when it came.'⁹

Once assured of an adequate income, the young middle class man and his wife could plan their expenditure appropriately, that is to say in accordance with certain expected standards of the day. A house of suitable size and location was the first requisite. Depending on the amount available for rent (about an eighth of total income was considered normal), this could vary from a six-roomed terrace house for the lowest paid clerks and book-keepers, to a substantial villa with ten or more rooms. Where servants lived in, ten rooms was about the minimum accommodation deemed adequate, say kitchen, dining-room, drawing-room, library, three family bedrooms, two servants' rooms and nursery, in addition to the hall, staircase and landing. Furnishings in the 1830s and 1840s were substantial, elegant and with an increasing emphasis on comfort. Mahogany was the favourite wood for furniture, which was hand made by cabinet makers. Carpets and curtains were much in evidence in all the family rooms, and bedrooms were equipped with elaborate toilet facilities – wash-stand with marble top, basin, ewer, chamber pots, brass hot water cans, and hip bath. There were as yet only a few signs of the clutter, fussiness and elaborate over-ornamentation which developed rapidly after the Great Exhibition of 1851 and which became for later generations the most indelible impression of Victorianism. Mr Pickwick's home at Dulwich ('fitted up with every attention to substantial comfort; perhaps to a little elegance besides') was an ideal to which many a middle class couple aspired at this time:

Everything was so beautiful! The lawn in front, the garden behind, the miniature conservatory, the dining-room, the drawing-room, the bed-rooms, the smoking-room, and above all the study with its pictures and easy chairs, and odd cabinets, and queer tables, and books out of number, with a large cheerful window opening upon a pleasant lawn and commanding a pretty landscape, just dotted here and there with little houses almost hidden by the trees; and then the curtains, and the carpets, and the chairs, and the sofas! Everything was so beautiful, so compact, so neat, and in such exquisite taste, said everybody, that there really was no deciding what to admire most.[10]

After the house and its furnishings came the other notable items of middle class expenditure: food, dress, carriages and domestic service. Books on domestic economy, with titles such as *Domestic Duties; or, Instructions to Young Married Ladies, on the Management of their Households*, and *The Book of Economy; or, How to Live Well in London on £100 per annum* appeared in increasing numbers, and were followed after 1848 by similar material in journals. Detailed planning and careful keeping of accounts became as normal for the middle classes in running their households as in their businesses. Calculation, economy and shrewd estimation of potential growth governed their household expenditure. Food and provisions, for instance, usually consumed 30 to 40 per cent of total income, but the standard of eating improved as prosperity increased. Alexis Soyer, a popular French chef of the 1840s, in his cookbook, *The Modern Housewife, or Ménagère* (1849), gave a series of weekly menus designed for different incomes. He presented these through the mouth of a Mrs B. of St John's Wood, whose husband began life as a small shopkeeper and progressed to a prosperous merchant.

'When I was first married,' recounted Mrs B., 'and commencing business, our means were limited: the following was our system of living:

Sunday's Dinner – Roast-Beef, Potatoes, Greens, and Yorkshire Pudding.

Monday – Hashed Beef and Potatoes.

Tuesday – Broiled Beef and Bones, Vegetables, and Spotted Dick Pudding.

Wednesday – Fish, if cheap, Chops, and Vegetables.

Thursday – Boiled Pork, Peas, Pudding, and Greens.

Friday – Peas Soup, remains of Pork.

Saturday – Stewed Steak with Suet Dumplings'.

After two years Mr B.'s business increased and three young clerks dined regularly with the family, so that Mrs B.'s culinary ideas (stimulated by a visit to France) became more ambitious. The weekly bill of fare was now as follows:

'*Sunday* – Pot-au-Feu, Fish – Haunch of Mutton, or a quarter of Lamb, or other good joint – Two Vegetables – Pastry and a Fruit Pudding – a little Dessert.

Monday – Vermicelli Soup made from the Pot-au-Feu of the day previous – The Bouilli of the Pot-au-Feu – Remains of the Mutton – Two Vegetables – Fruit Tart.

Tuesday – Fish – Shoulder of Veal Stuffed – Roast Pigeons, or Leveret or Curry – Two Vegetables – Apples with Rice, and light Pastry.

Wednesday – Spring Soup – Roast Fowls, Remains of Veal minced, and poached Eggs – Two Vegetables – Rowley Powley Pudding.

Thursday – Roast Beef – Remains of Fowl – Two Vegetables – Sweet Omelet.

Friday – Fish – Shoulder of Lamb – Mirotan of Beef – Two Vegetables – Baked Pudding.

Saturday – Mutton Broth – Broiled Neck of Mutton – Liver and Bacon – Two Vegetables – Currant Pudding'.

'At the present time,' explained Mrs B., 'we dine alone except when Mr B. invites somebody to dine with him, which is most generally the case: our daily bill of fare consists of something like the following: One Soup or Fish, generally alternate – One Remove, either Joint or Poultry – One Entrée – Two Vegetables – Pudding or Tart – A little Dessert.'

For a party of twelve persons Mrs B. would now provide something like this:

'*First Course*

One Soup, say Purée of Artichokes – One Fish, Cod Slices in Oyster Sauce – Remove with Smelts or White Bait.

Removes – Saddle of Mutton – Turkey in Celery Sauce.

Two Entrées – Cutlets à la Provençale – Sweetbreads larded in any White Sauce.

Two Vegetables – Greens – Kale – Potatoes on the Sideboard.

Second Course

Two Roasts – Partridges – Wild Ducks.

Jelly of Fruit – Cheesecakes – Meringue à la Crème – Vegetable – French Salad on the Sideboard.

Removes – Ice Pudding – Beignet Soufflé.
Dessert of eleven dishes.'[11]

Expenditure on dress, like the amount spent on food, could vary according to personal taste, and also (in the case of women) according to the ability to sew at home. The lower limits of this variety were set by notions of what was considered appropriate, for dress was an important indicator of status and calling. A member of the middle classes could never be mistaken for a labouring man or a lord: he just looked different. Fashions during the 1830s and 1840s tended to be discreet and unexaggerated: until 1836 both men's and women's dress was romantic and becoming, and the extravagant crinoline was not introduced until the 1850s. The model domestic budgets of the period usually allowed so much for rent, housekeeping and servants' wages, leaving the remainder to be spent on everything else, including dress. In general, dress was a matter of 'keeping up appearances'. This was even more true of expenditure on horses and carriages. For some types of calling, such as doctors, a carriage was a virtual necessity, but for a majority of the middle classes it was more important as a status symbol. Like automobiles in a later age, there were carriages to suit all pockets, from costly *barouches* to one-horse gigs. At least one horse and a coachman-groom had to be maintained and stables and coach-house provided. Such an expense could hardly be met out of an income under £600 a year. If one aspired to something grander, say a four-wheeled vehicle with two horses and footman, then a considerably larger income was required. In 1856 the number of people owning their own private carriages was slightly over 200,000. The horse and carriage were second only to land as symbols of social prestige derived from an aristocratic society. They survived the coming of the railway, and only succumbed (together with the cavalry) to the automobile in the First World War. For the lower middle classes, who could not afford a horse and carriage, the railways were a godsend, in that they offered cheap transport for work and leisure – a budgetary item that remained until ownership of a motor car became part of normal lower middle class aspiration.

The last main item of middle class expenditure – on domestic

The Railway – First Class

Second Class

Third Class

34 A fashionable picnic, with servants and wine, at Ascot races, 1844

35 High society, 1847

36 The latest fashions from
Paris, 1840

37 Famine scene in
Ireland, 1847

38 New shop fronts,
Regent Street,
London, 1846

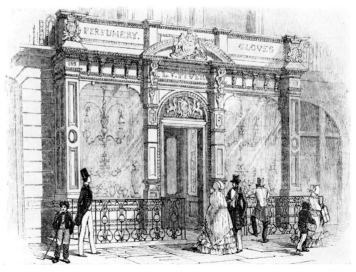

39 The Evil. Field Lane, London, said to have been the thieves' area described by Dickens in *Oliver Twist*

40 The Remedy. Model lodging house, St Giles, London

41 A very early photograph (dated 4 September 1854) of High Street, Wisbech, Cambridgeshire, showing a typical market town of the period

42-45 Labouring life in the countryside is vividly portrayed in these scenes of Dorsetshire in 1846:

42 General view of the village of Whitchurch

43 A typical labourer's cottage, near Blandford

44 Cottage interior

45 Dorsetshire labourers (wearing smocks) and their families

46 Anglican splendour: consecration of the Bishop of Manchester in Whitehall Chapel, 1848

47 Sunday worship in the Church of England. The Gothic church of St Andrews, Plymouth, has been virtually transformed into a meeting house, dominated by a huge central pulpit

48 Methodism in classical guise. Brunswick Wesleyan Methodist Chapel, Liverpool

49–50 Two contemporary woodcuts of the Plug riots, 1842: the conflict with the military at Preston (49) and the attack on the workhouse at Stockport (50)

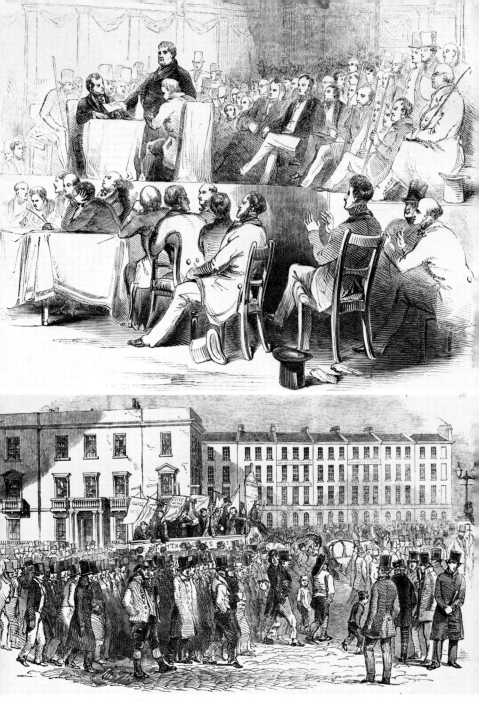

51 The decorum of middle class protest: an Anti-Corn Law League meeting, Covent Garden, London, 1844

52 The last great Chartist demonstration, 10 April 1848. The procession is here shown at Blackfriars Bridge, London

THE ROYAL NUPTIALS.

CAROUSAL OF GERMAN PAUPERS AT THE WEDDING BREAKFAST.

THE PRINCE *sings to the tune of* "*Auld lang syne.*"

Should old Jack Bull be e'er forgot?
No! drink his health in wine,
For thirty thousand pounds I've got,
And what is *her's* is mine!

(*Chorus.*)   Here's Garmany for ever, boys,
We make both Queens and Kings,
Large sausages and gilded toys,
And other *foolish things!*

Then here's success to Garmany,
To Vic. long life and health ;
My ragged pals in harmony,
She'll furnish soon with wealth !

(*Chorus.*)

THE QUEEN *drinks and sings.*

Here's health to John Bull, that jolly old fool,
Who has lavish'd his gold galore—
But nine months hence,
I'll have a young prince,
And then my dear friends he'll give more.

CHORUS, *by the company, to the air of* "*Tho' I leave thee now in sorrow.*"

We now leave this scene in sorrow ;
May we come again to-morrow ?
We would not start,
And e'er we part
A little English gold we'll borrow !

THE ENGLISH FLAG
AND THE
GERMAN RAG.

£30 000

£10 000

£3 000

£5 000

10 000

MEN'S SIDE

WOMENS SIDE

OLD SHOES KITCHEN STUFF

LEATHER APRONS

LEATHER BREECHES

BASTILE SOUP

A BLOW OUT FOR THE ENGLISH PAUPERS IN HONOUR OF THE ROYAL WEDDING DAY.

Russell.—The poor devils ought to have a treat upon such a day as this ; it will be a change for them.

Melbourne.—Rather an expensive one for the brutes, considering the rarity of the ingredients.

Bishop.—It smells delicious. I guess it is much too good for them.

Brougham.—Yes, it is feeding the pigs upon aldermen's fare : this is what I never intended when I suggested the Bastile Law.

CHORUS OF PAUPERS.

Let us all arise and join in the glee,
With a loud huzza, and three times three!
Huzza! we'll give the land we live in!
The glorious land we live in ! ! !
Huzza! huzza! huzza!

54 The way out: emigration. Dinner on an emigrant ship, 1844

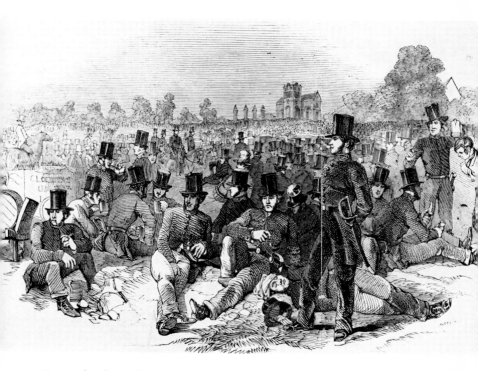

55 Law and order. Police at a Chartist demonstration in Bonners
Fields, London, June 1848

53 Anti-Poor Law satire (opposite), from the radical *Penny Satirist*, 1840

56 Interior of the court

PARKHURST PRISON, ISLE OF WIGHT, BUILT 1838

57 Prisoner's Cell   58 Officer and Prisoners

59 Andover Union workhouse, showing division into two separate halves for men and women

60 Visit of Prince Albert to a soup kitchen, Leicester Square, London, 1848

61 Sexual titillation, c.1830

CAN'T YOU LOOK THE OTHER WAY NOW

62 The Greek Slave, by the American sculptor, Hiram Power. The contemporary description of this highly popular exhibit at the Great Exhibition in 1851 explained that: 'the figure here represented is intended for that of a young and beautiful Greek girl, deprived of her clothing and exposed for sale to some wealthy eastern barbarian, before whom she is supposed to stand, with an expression of scornful dejection mingled with shame and disgust. Her dress, which is the modern Greek costume, appears on the column, and the cross implies her religion and country. The chains on her wrists are not historical, but have been added as necessary accessories.'

63 The Age of Steam. A tunnel near Bristol on the Great Western Railway, completed 1838–41

64 Chester station, 1840. Chester and Birkenhead Railway

65 Changing the face of the land. Crimple Valley viaduct, near Harrogate, 1847

66 Scene at the Bank of England, 1851

67 Experimental
electric light in
Trafalgar Square,
London, 1848

The first Shilling-day — going in.

The first Shilling-day — coming out

68 The cheap (shilling) day at the Great Exhibition, 1851

service – was in some ways the most crucial. At the end of the century when he carried out his great survey of working class poverty in York, Seebohm Rowntree still took the keeping or not of domestic servants as marking the division between the working and middle classes. The middle class was defined essentially as the servant-keeping class. Even the humblest house-holders in the lower middle classes expected to be able to have a servant of some kind, though she might be only a young girl of twelve or fourteen who made the fires and helped with the cleaning and washing. Many members of the middle class expected a good deal more, for a lavish use of domestic service was the chief means by which they used their incomes to increase their comfort and status. The number and types of domestic servants (who lived in the house and received board and lodging as well as wages) were regulated according to income. Below £300 per annum only a maid-of-all-work, perhaps assisted by a young girl, was possible. Above £300 another housemaid or a nursemaid could be added; and at £400 to £500 a cook could also be employed. There was general agreement in the domestic manuals that a complete household required the employment of at least three female servants, at a cost of £30 to £60 a year. Below this level, it was argued, the wife and daughters would be too involved in housework to cultivate those aspects of gentility to which they rightly aspired. Men servants (butlers, footmen, coachmen, grooms) were usually regarded as something of a luxury, though for 'carriage people' they were hardly avoidable. Except in rich households, a man servant, nominally called a butler, would be expected to undertake a number of duties, from general cleaning work to managing the cellar. A young man of the middle classes, unlike a labouring man, could reasonably expect his income to increase as he grew older, and therewith his social expectations. At the beginning of his married life he might be able to afford only a modest villa and one maid servant. But as he prospered his household would grow larger and more elabor-ate, and an increasingly large proportion of his income would be spent on domestic service.

The keeping of servants was for the middle classes more than just a matter of living comfortably or defining one's status within the ranks of superior persons. It went to the very heart of the idea of class itself. If, as has been suggested recently, class is not a thing or a category but a human relationship,[12] then Rowntree's drawing of the boundary between the working and middle classes in terms of the keeping or not of servants becomes a remarkably perceptive observation. The essence of middle classness was the experience of relating to other classes or orders in society. With one group, domestic servants, the middle classes stood in a very special and intimate relationship: the one in fact played an essential part in defining the identity of the other. Domestic servants were members of the household, with all the intimate relationships that living closely with other people entails. Yet they were excluded from the privileges of kinship and were always in a position of economic and social inferiority. Middle class domestic architecture provided the appropriate setting for this relationship. The typical town villa was much less spacious than the homes of the landed gentry, with the result that servants and employers were physically closer together. The house was designed vertically rather than horizontally, the servants occupying the basement and attics with the family living and sleeping on the floors between. Living in such close proximity was made tolerable for the middle classes only by the enforcement of strict rules and conventions governing all aspects of the daily routine. Mistresses very soon knew all the good and bad points of their cooks and maids, and conversely there can have been very few of the most intimate habits and attitudes of their masters and mistresses which were hidden from the servants. The children of the family were for most of the time consigned to the care of a nursemaid, or if they were still babies to a wet-nurse. Adolescent sons might be tempted (perhaps tacitly encouraged) into their first amorous adventures by the presence of an attractive housemaid. The result of all this intense and continuous experience was that the middle classes' relationship with their domestic servants was complex and ambiguous. Servants were both indispensable to the middle class as a class, and at the same time were the Greatest Plague of Life.

Such was the title of a comic volume by Henry and Augustus Mayhew published in 1847, describing 'the adventures of a lady in search of a good servant'. Needless to say the lady was anything but successful. Her ideal of a real 'treasure' was clear: a respectable middle-aged woman who would work for £10 a year 'and find her own tea and sugar'; and who moreover

had a ten years' excellent character from her last situation, which had been with a clergyman in the country. She was cleanly, even tempered, an early riser, a good plain cook, and a devout Christian; she was honest, industrious and sober; in fact, she had just taken the pledge.[13]

The lady soon discovered that these qualities were the very opposite of those possessed by a succession of servants whom it was her misfortune to hire. After fourteen years' housekeeping (during which 'I cannot say the creatures have let me know one day's perfect peace'), she and her husband decided to retire to a respectable boarding house 'to taste a little peace and quiet and comfort, for the first time since my marriage'. The humour of the book derives from the social pretensions of the lower middle class narrator and her gullibility in being deceived by the various types of dishonest and inefficient servants who impose upon her. This genre became popular in the 1840s; and jokes about 'the Servant Problem' took their place beside class snobbery and the Irish in the pages of *Punch*, where the middle classes sought a weekly catharsis from their social obsessions.

The pattern of middle class expenditure, together with one of its important implications, is brought out in the satirical poem *Three Hundred Pounds a Year* by Eliza Cook, a popular writer of the 1840s and 1850s. A young man, addressing his beloved, regrets that much as he adores her he cannot afford to marry with only £300 a year.

> Sweet girl! you know three hundred pounds
> Would prove a slender axis
> For household wheels to run their rounds
> In yearly rent and taxes.
> You see, dear, that our home *must* be
> Out West, about the squares,

With good reception rooms – full three•
And servants' flight of stairs.
You *must* have '*soirées*' now and then
(Though *I* can't see *their* use);
And *I must* often have some men
To dinner – '*à la Russe*'.
I've asked my uncle for his aid;
Of course, he wont accord it;
And so our bliss must be delayed,
For means, love, wont afford it.

A housemaid, cook, and liveried boy
We must, at once engage;
One of the two we must employ –
A footman, or a page.
I cannot well resign at 'Lord's',
And you, dear Flo, of course,
Must go to balls and make your 'calls
With decent brougham and horse.
I must keep up my name at 'White's'
Despite all uncle says;
You still must have your opera nights
And show on Chiswick days.
Now, if I had three thousand, dear,
You know I would not hoard it;
But on three *hundred* pounds a year!
I really can't afford it.

In order to maintain an appropriate middle class standard of living, young men were advised to postpone marriage until they could afford the trappings necessary to their status. Thus was the Malthusian doctrine of prudential restraint converted to the use of middle class ideology.

Central to all the aspects of middle class life which we have so far considered was the cult of the home and the sanctity of the family. Fed by authors like Eliza Cook, sentimentality gathered thickly round the ideas of Mother and Home. Her very popular poem, *The Old Arm-Chair* (1837) began thus:

I love it, I love it; and who shall dare
To chide me for loving that old Arm-chair?

> I've treasured it long as a sainted prize;
> I've bedewed it with tears, and embalmed it with sighs.

The image of the cosy hearth, round which the family gathered regularly, was repeated endlessly in poems and magazine articles. (This was perhaps making a virtue out of necessity, given the absence of central heating and the consequent need to sit near the fire to keep warm, and may explain the national hobby of poking the fire.) Home was especially a private place, where the individual could retire from the stresses and strains of the busy world. Windows were heavily curtained to frustrate the prying eyes of strangers: gardens were surrounded by high brick walls to preserve privacy from neighbours. Home was also a comfortable place, and the arts of domesticity were highly regarded. In no previous age had domestic manuals provided such lengthy and detailed instructions on how to make a bed, lay a fire or dust a sitting-room. These were not trivial matters, to be left to chance or inherited wisdom, but important aspects of domestic comfort which every middle class housewife should teach her servants. Furniture, especially those pieces designed for the masculine (that is, dining and smoking) rooms, emphasised comfort before elegance; an upholstered easychair in which the master of the house could lounge was an essential part of the philosophy of home. Such was the dominance of the cult of home that domestic virtue extended to literature and the fine arts. Novels and plays had to be such as a father could read aloud to his wife and daughters without embarrassment – following the example of the egregious Dr Thomas Bowdler who in 1818 had published a *Family Shakespeare* from which all 'improper' passages had been removed. Paintings were expected to be didactic and, above all, moral. Favourite artists were those who painted warm, sentimental subjects with great attention to realistic detail, such as Edwin Landseer, whose animal scenes were highly admired by the Queen and Prince Albert. The ultimate triumph of domesticity was its capture of the very monarchy itself. In the persons of Victoria and Albert the nation saw, not the apex of a feudal aristocratic order, but a bourgeois family on the throne. This, as Bagehot observed, was 'an interesting idea', since it brought down 'the pride of sovereignty to the level of petty life'.

The cosy, comfortable, private home provided the setting in which was embowered the middle class family. This institution, unlike its working class counterpart, emerged in early Victorian Britain as a well-defined, stable and confident part of society – an example to labouring men and aristocrats alike. Although much of our knowledge (and most of our stereotypes) of the middle class family come from the mid and late Victorian periods, the main pattern of its development was already clear by the 1840s. An important problem here is to distinguish between the Victorians' ideal of home and family and the reality. In the idealised version of the family its claims were pitched very high; it was a holy institution. Charles Kingsley, an Anglican parson and Christian Socialist of the 1848 vintage, believed that human family relationships were 'given us to teach us their divine antitypes': 'fully to understand the meaning of "a Father in Heaven" we must be fathers ourselves; to know how Christ loved the Church, we must have wives to love, and love them'.[14] The Victorians knew, as well as their critics of a later generation, that in fact the home was often far from being a temple, despite the family prayers every evening and attendance at church on Sunday morning. What was distinctive and significant about the middle class home and family in the 1840s was not that the actual life of its members was greatly different from the previous generation, but that the idea of family life was changing. R.H.Tawney once remarked that social institutions are the visible expression of the scale of moral values which rules the minds of individuals.[15] The middle classes took the ancient institution of the family, invested it with new powers and assigned new roles to its various members, in accordance with their social and moral philosophy. It is this image of what the middle classes thought the ideal should be that passes, for most people today, as the typical Victorian family. If this is a distorted and incomplete image, to which no actual family more than partially approximated, it nevertheless highlights those features of the early Victorian family which are felt to be remote (either in time or sentiment) from us today.

The middle class family was a strictly hierarchical group with the husband at its head. There could be little doubt about his authority over all other members – wife, children, servants – for his effective economic control was backed up by legal sanctions. Unlike the labouring family, to which several of its members might contribute their earnings, the middle class family was dependent on the income of its head alone: middle class wives and children did not go out to work, and any property a wife possessed was legally her husband's. Children were expected to subordinate themselves to their parents. When young they were to be seen and not heard; and when they were older they remained financially dependent on their father until they had begun to make their way in business or, if girls, had married. For wives the Pauline injunction was absolute: 'Wives, be in subjection unto your own husbands ... for the husband is the head of the wife, as Christ also is the head of the Church'. Servants too had little option but to obey St Paul ('Servants, be obedient unto them that according to the flesh are your masters'), for their whole position was based on the assumption of deference. As an effective instrument of social discipline the middle class family had few equals. It exerted a pressure for social conformity which was all but overwhelming and which extended ultimately throughout most of society. But this outward success was only achieved at a price, and the internal stresses and strains of family life were seldom far below the surface. Relations between husband and wife, and between parents and children; the regulation of sexual *mores*; and the position of 'old maids', were all sources of tension and potential unhappiness. In the idealised version, of course, these strains were covered over, so that from the outside the early Victorian family seemed an oasis of happiness in an often-cruel world; but sometimes such a home could be a veritable prison.

For women the middle class family provided a strangely restricted and debilitating role. Dependent on her husband, whom she did not see all day, relieved of many of the old household chores by servants, and barred by the conventions of 'refinement' from all but a few occupations such as sewing, embroidery or playing the pianoforte, the middle class wife had difficulty in avoiding a life of utter triviality and boredom. True the domestic manuals outlined a daily routine of busy supervision of the household and bringing up the children: and Mrs Sarah Stickney Ellis in her incomparable *Women of England* (1839), assured her female readers that 'a nation's moral wealth is in your keeping'. But it is clear that not all women were content to accept this role, with its complete subordination of all else to the pursuit of marriage and the claims of family. Florence Nightingale, who refused an offer of marriage, commented in 1851: 'Women don't consider themselves as human beings at all, there is absolutely no God, no country, no duty to them at all, except family'.[16] Once married, a middle class woman was securely within a gilded cage from which there was no escape. Divorce was virtually impossible until 1857, and for many years thereafter the divorce court was little used. A wife was expected to be personally submissive to her husband, sexually as well as socially. She was not supposed to desire sexual intercourse for any pleasure she might derive from it, but solely as a duty to her husband and the need for procreation. The socially-approved model of female sexuality was devised by men and accepted by a majority of women. The burden of successive (and unwanted) pregnancies was not the least of the bonds which disadvantaged wives. Queen Victoria, replying to the King of the Belgians, in 1841, wrote:

> I think, dearest Uncle, you cannot *really* wish me to be the 'Maman d'une nombreuse famille', for I think you will see with me the great inconvenience a *large* family would be to us all, and particularly to myself; men never think, at least seldom think, what a hard task it is for us women to go through this *very often*.[17]

Nevertheless, she went on, 'God's will be done'; and before the early death of the Prince Consort in 1861 she had borne him nine children. No wonder that Alfred Tennyson in his poem *The Queen* (1851) addressed her as 'Mother, Wife, and Queen' – in that order.

Equally difficult was the role of single women in the middle class family; and the statistics cited in Chapter One suggest that this was a sizable problem.[18] For girls whose education was finished (and it was perfunctory compared with their brothers' schooling at a local grammar or public school), there was little to fill their heads but thoughts of marriage. Barred from taking up any occupation outside the home, ignorant of the physiology of sex and full of romantic notions of love, they could only wait for their husband-to-be to appear. 'Daughters,' wrote Florence Nightingale, 'can only have a choice among those people whom their parents like, and who like their parents well enough to come to their house.'[19] Not many women in the 1840s had the strength or inclination to do as Florence Nightingale did, and deliberately chose a single life and a career outside the home, even though an unknown number may have harboured secret resentments against their lot. Marriage was the most socially-approved goal for women; and the pressures for conformity and the repressive power of the middle class family were here put fully into operation. Moreover, there was in most families a constant reminder of the unhappy alternative to marriage: the spectre of the middle-aged spinster. Her role was anything but enviable. If she lived in her brother's or sister's home she could not do much in the way of housekeeping because this would encroach on the wife's prerogative: the most she could aspire to was teaching the smaller children and acting as a 'companion' to her sister. If she lived with her aged parents she had to combine the functions of nurse and housekeeper without being mistress of the house. A third possibility was to go as a governess to some affluent family, but this was to accept a position as a rather superior kind of servant. The way in which early Victorians looked at the role of unmarried women came out in the discussions beginning in 1835 over the question of marriage with a deceased wife's sister. A bill to legalise such unions was introduced in 1841, but the issue dragged on through the rest of the century (with the bench of bishops, in W. S. Gilbert's quip, concerned to

>   ... prick that annual blister
> Marriage to deceased wife's sister.)

The opponents of reform argued that it would destroy marital morals if the sexual taboo on sisters-in-law were removed: once a wife's sister could be looked on as an attractive, marriageable person by the husband, his relationship to her and hers to him would be quite changed. Husbands would be tempted to put away their wives and seduce their sisters-in-law, who in turn would see themselves as supplanters in their sisters' beds. It would be impossible (because offensive to delicacy and purity) for maiden maternal aunts to live in their sisters' homes any more.

The significance of such fears lay not in whether they were soundly based nor whether any substantial number of people was likely to be affected by the reform, but in the assumptions about sexual behaviour that were implied. The middle class family sought to regulate and control sexual relationships, but it was only partially successful. Repression and obscurantism ultimately brought their own nemesis. Sex was unmentionable in the early Victorian home, and children's questions about it were turned aside, so that they grew up puzzled, ignorant and resentful. The ideal of chastity and the practice of prudery were the defences of the middle class family against the pressures of sexuality. With women and children this coercive discipline was largely effective in repressing outward manifestations of the sexual impulse and channelling sexual relationships in socially acceptable directions. But with men the degree of success was smaller: hence the tacit admission of a double standard of sexual morality.

For the young middle class male the early Victorian family constituted a combination of social, economic and sexual disciplines to which he sometimes found it impossible to submit. He had been brought up to expect a fairly comfortable standard of living, but his commencing salary was often inadequate for such a standard unless he could live at home. Anthony Trollope's first seven years (1834–41) in London as a young clerk in the General Post Office, was a period of impecuniosity. 'During the whole of this time,' he wrote, 'I was hopelessly in debt.' Living in cheap lodgings, with no friend to help or advise him, he led an uncomfortable and drab existence.

There was no house in which I could habitually see a lady's face and hear a lady's voice. No allurement to decent respectability came in my way. It seems to me that in such circumstances the temptations of loose life will almost certainly prevail with a young man.[20]

In Trollope's case there is no evidence that his 'loose life' amounted to more than youthful rowdiness and squalor, but for others in similar circumstances it could have meant sexual profligacy. Trollope did not marry until 1844, when he was twenty-nine, thus exercising admirable Malthusian prudential restraint in delaying marriage until he could support a wife and family. This was model middle class behaviour. How many young men followed this exemplar we have no way of knowing; perhaps a majority did. But certainly many did not: delay in marriage accompanied by sexual continence was not felt by them to be tolerable.

At this point the discipline of the family was put under severe strain. To avoid an open breakdown some subterfuge, some accommodation was necessary. Within the structure of the middle class home this was not easy to arrange. The inviolability of female chastity was so fiercely protected, the penalties on 'fallen women' so great, and ignorance of contraceptive techniques so complete, that pre- or extra-marital intercourse with middle class wives and daughters was not a practicable solution to the problem. More latitude was possible with female domestic servants, and there is some evidence that this afforded a certain measure of relief. The anonymous middle class author of *My Secret Life* described how his first sexual experiences (probably in the 1830s or 1840s) were with the maids in his mother's home, and he quickly discovered that 'servants are fair game' for the sexual adventurer. A common theme in Victorian novels is the seduction of a working girl by the son of an affluent family. William Acton, a doctor who practised in London from 1840, noted in his book on *Prostitution* (1857) that 'seduction of girls [from the lower orders] is a sport and a habit with vast numbers of men, married . . . and single, placed above the ranks of labour'. The relationship between sex and social class displayed here is a mixture of brutality and exploitation on the one side and deference and the temptations that stem from poverty on the other.

The main solution of the problem, however, came from elsewhere. Prostitution was referred to by the Victorians as the Great Social Evil. Reliable estimates of the numbers of prostitutes are notoriously hard to come by, but the *Westminster Review* in 1850 gave a conservative figure of eight thousand in London and fifty thousand for England and Scotland. Bracebridge Hemyng in Mayhew's fourth volume of *London Labour and the London Poor* was prepared to put the number as high as eighty thousand for London alone. Whatever the exact figure, the business of prostitution was large and visible in all large cities – much more so than in Britain today. Prostitutes ranged from the kept mistresses of wealthy businessmen and aristocrats to common harlots who solicited on the streets. The majority were from the lower orders, part of the world of those who would not work. Acton estimated that in London there was at least one prostitute to every eighty-one adult males, and in Edinburgh the proportion was about the same. How many clients each prostitute had daily or weekly we do not know. But Acton, who was far from being an alarmist, concluded that 'prostitution diffuses itself through the social fabric, though it is perceptible for a time only'. And he added: 'I repeat that prostitution is a transitory state, through which an untold number of British women are ever on their passage'.[21]

Behind the early Victorian family, and essential for the maintenance of its facade, was the great underworld of prostitution. A relationship of mutual dependence linked the two institutions together; they were in fact the obverse and reverse of the same coin. The reality was covered over, the subject was made socially unmentionable, and the middle classes tried to pretend that it did not exist. No novelist dared openly allude to the subject, yet it is clear that Charles Dickens knew all about it and that his Victorian gentlemen readers would recognise Nancy in *Oliver Twist* (even without Dickens' admission in the preface to later editions) as a prostitute. From the early 1840s there was a steady output of books and articles on prostitution and sexual disorders, though these did little to change the general climate of opinion and were mainly of use to social reformers and philanthropists. This social myopia, or attempt to erase from the middle class consciousness all knowledge of sexually unacceptable behaviour has caused later generations to charge the Victorians with hypocrisy. But in fact it was a usual reaction of any society faced with a threat to one of its basic institutions. To restore confidence in itself society pushes the offending behaviour out of sight, at the same time tacitly allowing it to continue as a safety valve. In this way the early Victorians created a kind of invisible sub-society – invisible physically in that it was confined to certain known areas of the town, and invisible mentally in that it was expunged from social and personal consciousness.

It is in relation to this underworld of prostitution and crime that the middle class concepts of respectability, purity and prudery become meaningful. They were fences erected by a superior social class to mark itself off from, and to protect itself against, an inferior culture. The patterns of poverty could not be allowed to undermine the patterns of prosperity; rather should it be the other way round. The relationship between the affluent and the poor was nevertheless far from simple. Their life styles were in many ways far apart (compare the menus cited in this chapter with the diet of the labouring poor in Chapter Two), yet at certain points they reacted upon each other. The middle classes needed the labouring poor not only economically as a work force, but also socially and even sexually, as a means of establishing their own identity. The poor accepted the employee-employer relationship between themselves and the middle and gentry classes, but also looked upon them as objects of deference. The social and psychological bonds of early Victorian society managed to hold it together; though, as we shall see later, they were subjected to greater strains than perhaps ever before.

5
Early Victorian Values

The Map of Religion: Church and Chapel

The early Victorian era was essentially a religious age. Whether it was also more spiritual than earlier or succeeding ages is by no means so clear, though charges of hypocrisy are not now assumed so readily as in the days of the 1920s reaction to all things Victorian. The present chapter is not concerned with theology or ecclesiastical organisation, but rather with some aspects of the influence of religion upon the daily lives and social attitudes of the people. How effective was religion as a form of social control; to what extent did Christian beliefs and values relate to social action? These and similar questions can only be answered after we have taken a look at the map of religion. Men seldom have single-minded motives for their social activities, and in the 1830s and 1840s religious values and allegiances coloured most social issues, either directly or in more subtle ways.

Probably the most striking difference in this respect between the early Victorian period and our own age was the extent of outward religious observance. In 1851, for the first and only time, an official census of attendance at all places of religious worship was taken.[1] It showed that on Sunday, 30 March 1851, over seven million of the eighteen million inhabitants of England and Wales attended public worship. After allowing for young children, invalids and aged persons, and those who were occupied in household and other work on Sundays (totalling about 30 per cent of the population who could not attend church or chapel), it was estimated that about 60 per cent of possible worshippers attended, and 40 per cent did not. When these overall figures are broken down they reveal something of the pattern of religious worship in 1851. Attendance in rural areas and small towns was noticeably higher than in large towns of more than 10,000 people. Most of the absentees lived in the large towns of the industrial areas. As between different denominations, the Church of England was shown to be strongest in the villages and country towns, the Nonconformists in certain of the recently-expanded towns of the 'chief manufacturing districts'.

If to a later generation it is the high proportion of church and chapel attenders which is impressive, to contemporaries it was the non-attenders who created most concern. Despite the strict sabbatarianism and regular church or chapel going which was enjoined by powerful groups in all denominations, it was obvious that religion did not have a very firm hold on a large part of the population. The number of attenders at services seemed but small when compared with the number of sittings available in the churches and chapels. Thus in Leeds (with a population of 172,270 in 1851) which had a total of 76,488 sittings in all its places of worship, the number of worshippers at the most numerously attended morning services was 39,392. In particular the working classes were most obviously absent. 'In cities and large towns,' wrote Horace Mann, who was the author of the official report on the census, 'it is observable how absolutely insignificant a portion of the congregations is composed of artisans.' Although in their youth they attended National, British and Sunday schools, when once they began full time labour they 'soon become as utter strangers to religious ordinances as the people of a heathen country'. In his report Mann mentioned several possible causes of this; but they were all only different facets of a central conviction, widely held among labouring men, that religious services were primarily for the middle classes; and that the social gulf which separated them from what Bagehot called 'the scriptural classes' could not be bridged in the ordinary place of public worship. The census results hammered home what had already become clear to many ministers and concerned laymen, namely, that the churches by and large were basically middle class institutions. 'British Christianity,' declared Edward Miall in the *Nonconformist* in 1849, 'is essentially the Christianity developed by a middle class soil.'[2]

The indifference or hostility of working men towards the Church of England is not difficult to explain. Politically the Anglican clergy were unpopular because they adhered more faithfully than any other group to the high Tory party in the days of its decline. Intellectually the Erastianism of the church aroused nothing but contempt in the minds of working class reformers. Socially the gulf between a vicar with an income of as much as £1,000 a year and a handloom weaver with 12s a week if he were lucky, was felt to be too great to allow of any common interests. It was not necessary to be a Dissenter to feel repelled by the abuses within the church. Richard Oastler, a Tory-Anglican, was moved to protest against the attempts of a new vicar of Halifax to increase his tithe revenues when his income was already £1,500 a year. At the other extreme were the 5,230 curates in England and Wales whose average annual stipend amounted to only £81. Neither of the two main forms of Church of England Christianity was such as to make much appeal to ordinary working people in the 1830s. The latitudinarian tradition made the church appear as nothing but a worldly, expensive anachronism; and the original saintliness of the earlier Evangelicals had been lost when Evangelicalism became respectable and fashionable. If the church were to make any significant impact on the working classes – or on many of the industrial middle classes – it clearly required a new approach. Thomas Arnold, the famous headmaster of Rugby School, writing in 1832 commented:

Phrases which did well enough formerly, now only excite a sneer; it does not do to talk to the operatives about our 'pure and apostolic church', and 'our glorious constitution'; they have no respect for either; but one must take higher ground. . . . The church as it now stands, no human power can save.[3]

But from about 1836 signs of change within the Church of England became apparent. The Victorian church which then began to emerge was marked by energy and strength. In rural areas a good deal of the old social tradition, shorn of its worst abuses, continued among the 'Barsetshire' clergy. But in the towns a new figure – the slum parson – began to emerge; and in the industrial areas Anglican champions of social reform appeared side by side with Chartists and radicals. New parishes, archdeaconries, and dioceses were created in industrial districts. By 1850 evidence of new life within the church was abundantly clear. There was a veritable spate of repairing old churches and building new ones. School building, and the formation of guilds, sisterhoods and charities, were indicative of a new fervour in parochial work. After 1845 the repercussions of the Tractarian movement (a Catholic revival within the Church of England, originally centred in Oxford) were felt in a more devout attitude towards the liturgy and ceremonial of the church, in the more frequent celebration of the Holy Communion, and in the observation of Holy Days and Seasons. Perhaps of greatest significance in its social effects was the new conception of the role of the church in the community. If this was interpreted by Thomas Arnold to mean a Christian scholar and gentleman in every parish, the other side of the medal was portrayed in the Rev. J.J.Blunt's little manual, *The Duties of the Parish Priest*, with its emphasis on obligations towards the parishioners.

As Arnold's phrase suggested, the gulf between the rectory and the cottage was to remain as great as ever. What was new was the insistence that the middle classes, lay and clerical, had a duty towards the labouring population. Contemporaries never used the word guilt, but the hum of evangelical fervour in a multitude of organisations for good works after 1836, suggests that some such feeling was perhaps subconsciously implicit in the relation between the middle classes and the poor. Clothing clubs, soup kitchens, parochial schools were alike products, in some degree, of this relationship.

It was in the industrial areas that the new type of Anglican, whether parson or layman, marked the greatest break with the immediate past. Richard Oastler, who campaigned against the brutalities of child slavery in Yorkshire mills, and urged fierce resistance to the New Poor Law, had left the Methodist Church of his childhood to join the Church of England. The Reverend

George Stringer Bull, vicar of Bierley, championed the same causes through the 1830s. By far the most influential of the new type of Anglican clergyman in Yorkshire was the Reverend Dr Walter Farquhar Hook, vicar of Leeds from 1837 to 1859. The fortunes of the church in Leeds were at a low ebb when Hook began his ministry there. It was his achievement that he, a High Churchman in the midst of a strongly evangelical community, rehabilitated the Church of England in the eyes of the middle classes, and won the respect and even the affection of many of the working classes. That he earned the epithet of 'the working man's vicar' was due largely to his obvious and sincere concern for projects of social reform. His open support of the ten hours movement, the early closing movement, and the development of public parks, together with his active work for popular education, ranged him on the side of working class reformers. His social philosophy, like Oastler's, was Tory-Radicalism, with its ideal of the well-being of the whole of society and not just of one class. It was a conscious attempt to make Christianity relevant to industrial society.

Nevertheless, even the most sympathetic 'working man's vicar' was far removed socially from his working class flock. No one ever suggested that a labouring man might become a vicar; the ideal of a scholar and gentleman in every parish made such an idea preposterous. If the working classes, or indeed many of the middle classes, desired a closer identification with the organisation and control of the church they had to turn elsewhere. Hence it was in the various Nonconformist churches that many of them found a more congenial religious home. Despite the herculean labours of Hook in Leeds, the dominant religious ethos of the West Riding was essentially one of Dissent. Shortly after his arrival in Leeds in 1837 Hook perceived this clearly.

The real fact is [he wrote] that the established religion in Leeds is Methodism, and it is Methodism that all the most pious among the churchmen unconsciously talk. If you ask a poor person the ground of his hope, he will immediately say that he feels he is saved, however great a sinner he may be.[4]

It was then eighty-five years since Methodism had been first introduced into Leeds by John Nelson, a stonemason of Birstal, who had been converted after hearing John Wesley preach at Moorfields in 1739. By 1851, out of a total of 983,423 attendances made on census Sunday in Yorkshire, over 600,000 were at Dissenting places of worship, and of these 431,000 were at Methodist chapels of various sorts.

The Methodist body in the first half of the nineteenth century, however, was by no means homogeneous, and the social and political allegiances of Methodists were divided along the lines of Disraeli's Two Nations. As long as John Wesley himself was alive the Methodists generally took little active part in politics, but after his death in 1791 the official political neutrality of the central organisation, the Wesleyan Conference, became increasingly, in effect, political conservatism. The growing wealth of many middle class members of the societies, and the consequent desire to be considered respectable, naturally inclined them to shun anything which might carry the taint of radicalism or disloyalty, especially in the period after 1815. By the 1830s there was added to this negative instinct a positive desire to support the political and social programmes of the middle classes, of which many of them were members. Wesleyan mill owners and businessmen were not prepared to remain neutral on social and political issues which affected them closely.

Underlying the dominant conservatism of official Methodism was a liberal and democratic spirit. From the time when John Wesley took to preaching salvation in the open air and humble men were converted, Methodism was a popular movement, and most of the schisms which rent the central Wesleyan body until 1849 were attempts, in one form or another, to reassert this basic characteristic. The break-away churches (such as the Methodist New Connexion (1796), the Primitive Methodists (1811), the Bible Christians (1815), the Protestant Methodists (1827), the Barkerites (1841), the Wesleyan Reformers (1849)) were characterised by differences of organisation and personalities, not of doctrine. Methodism, unlike the Church of England, was essentially a layman's religion. In addition to the full-time ministers (who had the superintendence of a number of chapels in a circuit), there was an army of active lay helpers, numbering in 1850 some 20,000 local preachers, over 50,000 class leaders, together with trustees, stewards, prayer leaders and Sunday school teachers. How many of these were working men is difficult to ascertain, and the class composition of Methodism differed between connexions and between individual chapels in the same connexion. At the two extremes of the social scale – among the aristocracy and the non-respectable labouring poor – Methodism had little influence; but among the middle classes and some sections of the working classes it secured a firm hold. While the Wesleyan Methodists in most places were predominantly a middle class body, the Primitive Methodists had a pronounced working class flavour. In some of the industrial towns and villages of the Midlands, and in rural areas too, the Primitive Methodists successfully pioneered a type of religion adapted to the needs of labouring men and women. Thus in the East Riding of Yorkshire a Primitive Methodist circuit was established at Driffield in 1837, after which societies in the villages on the Wolds multiplied rapidly. Farm labourers attended the 'Ranters' ' meetings, held in a crowded cottage or plain, humble village chapel, and listened to a local preacher who was himself a working man and spoke their idiom. They felt at home there in a way they seldom did in the parish church with its liturgy, ritual and sermon by a middle class parson.

There are other types of evidence of the impact of Methodism at a popular level. It is not an accident that almost every self-educated working man in early and mid Victorian England, who came to write his memoirs, paid tribute to the beneficial influences of Methodism in his youth. The accounts of self-educated men show a pattern of Methodist domestic piety, help in a local Sunday school, conversion, membership of a Methodist class, preaching, and then (usually) a progression beyond the original Methodism to some new intellectual position. Methodism for them was almost a natural stage in their educational and moral development; and for thousands of less distinguished labouring men and women it remained an intellectual and philosophical resting place. Joseph Barker, the son of a Bramley (Leeds) handloom

weaver was brought up in his father's trade.⁵ At the age of six
or seven he was already a 'believer in the great doctrines of
religion', and his Methodist parents brought him up to look for
salvation through conversion. After attending Sunday school he
became a member of a Methodist class, and was helped in his
studies by a Methodist travelling preacher stationed at Bramley
and also by a local schoolmaster who was a Methodist local
preacher. Barker himself became a local preacher for the Wesleyan
Methodists while still working as a handloom weaver, but after
a time joined the Methodist New Connexion, becoming first a
travelling preacher and later a chapel minister. In 1841 he was
expelled from that Connexion, taking with him some twenty-
nine chapels and over four thousand members, mostly in the
West Riding. Thereafter he progressed through several different
religious positions and became a radical journalist.

The impact which Methodism made upon working men was
complex. In so far as it inculcated the goals of respectability and
hard work it reinforced the puritan values of the middle classes.
The convenience of religion as a work discipline was not lost
upon contemporaries. But the popular roots of Methodism also
meant that it could contribute to some of the working class
movements described in the next chapter. The Methodist class
system provided a useful model for Chartist and radical organisation, and a class or band meeting could as easily study the
works of Thomas Paine as the Old Testament. Camp meetings
and chapels were institutions which could serve secular as well as
religious purposes, and the eloquence and self-discipline acquired
through preaching from a chapel pulpit was a useful training
for addressing mass meetings of Chartists or Short Timers. As
schools of practical democracy and self-government the Methodist
chapels rendered valuable service to popular movements. Not only
did working men utilise directly Methodist forms and techniques
for other causes, but they also assimilated Methodist thought
and attitudes into movements for social and political reform.
Life for the working man was not to be lived in separate com-
partments; his religion and his social strivings had to be harmonised. Nor was this a very difficult task, for religious sanction

for most radical opinions could be found in the pages of the New Testament. At the great Chartist meeting at Peep Green on Whit Monday, 1839,

the proceedings opened with prayer by Mr William Thornton, at the close of which Feargus O'Connor put his hand on his shoulder and said, 'Well done, Thornton, when we get the People's Charter I will see that you are made the Archbishop of York'.[6]

Thornton, a leading West Riding Chartist, was a Methodist local preacher; and the writer of this description, Ben Wilson, was also a Chartist and a member of the Wesleyan chapel at Salterhebble.

No other group of nonconformists had such a large following among the working classes as the Methodists. The Old Dissent (that is, the churches descended from the sects of the seventeenth century) was predominantly middle class in membership and outlook, with the exception of certain Baptist chapels in the industrial North and in Wales. When the Old Dissenters wished to establish contact with the working classes they had to make a conscious effort to go out to them. Thus the Unitarians in Leeds and Liverpool established Domestic Missions in the 1840s to further their work among the labouring poor. When the Society of Friends began their Sabbath schools at the same time, it was a venture in which the initiative came from a small group of prosperous middle class evangelicals; and although it was very successful in establishing educational and social contacts with the labouring population of Birmingham, York and other towns, very few of these working class students ever became Quakers. In the Congregational chapels the middle class element likewise predominated. The artisan who felt out of place, socially and spiritually, in an Anglican church, was likely to feel scarcely less of a stranger in the company of wealthy industrialists in their large and fashionable down-town chapels. While the Old Dissent did not make the same type of direct appeal to sections of the working classes as did Methodism, its influence nevertheless was often in a direction sympathetic to working class advance. An important minority in the leadership of the Old Dissenting bodies was radically inclined towards social and political change; and could usually be counted on to support specific demands on questions of popular education, extension of the suffrage, and attacks on ancient privilege.

Also classified as a sect by most early Victorians, was the Roman Catholic church. Since the Reformation the Catholics in England and Scotland had been reduced to a small, sometimes persecuted group which had played little part in the national life; but in Ireland a majority of the population adhered to the old faith. With the Irish immigration the situation in Great Britain was radically changed. Instead of a church composed of a few ancient landed families, mostly in the North, the Roman communion became a body catering to the needs of predominantly working class congregations of Irish origin. So rapidly did the numbers grow, that in 1850 the Roman hierarchy was reintroduced into Great Britain (amidst enraged Protestant and Anglican protests at the Papal Aggression), and a small but highly distinguished flow of converts from the Tractarians added a leaven of English intellectual respectability.

Beyond the world of what may be called respectable religion lay a sub-culture of popular religion, about which historians at present know very little. No hard and fast line can be drawn between the various brands of orthodoxy and the adventist and millenarian sects which flourished in different parts of the country. From Anglicanism and Wesleyanism, through Primitive Methodism and revivalism there was a gradual shading off into the more extreme forms of Protestant sectarianism.

Some of these sects were native to Great Britain, like the Plymouth Brethren, the Southcottians (followers of the prophet-ess, Joanna Southcott, who died in 1814) and their offshoot the Wroeites or Christian Israelites. Others came from abroad, like the Swedenborgians, the Millerites, and the Mormons (who were strong in Lancashire and the Potteries in the 1840s). A local prophet or messiah had little difficulty in gathering round him a coterie of devoted followers – witness the strange episode of 'Sir William Courtenay', a millennialist who claimed to be the Messiah and who died fighting against the military in Kent in 1838. Carlyle in his essay, *Signs of the Times* (1829), referred to the contemporary 'rage of prophecy', and throughout the 1830s and 1840s there was much reference to an approaching crisis and the millennium. How large this 'underworld' of popular religion was we do not know; little of it appears in the 1851 census. But it is clear that the membership of these sects, together with the non-Wesleyan Methodist chapels, constituted a religious element among people untouched by the orthodox churches. In the special values of sectarianism they found something that they needed and which they could not find elsewhere in early Victorian society. Membership of an intelligible and familiar community, where they could feel that their talents were fully valued; a sense of separateness from the world, a common experience of conversion, and a shared belief in their special mission to preach the kingdom and prepare for the second advent; a congenial home, where the values and goals were different from those of the wider society, and where unbounded hopes of a future millennium could be indulged – these were the qualities found in a multitude of Little Bethels, Mount Zions and Zoars.

Yet wider than all formal religious institutions, whether popular or respectable, was the influence of nonconformist Christianity which coloured the thinking of members of the middle and working classes. The desire for a religion free from credal beliefs, conceding the right of private judgement, and unconnected with any ecclesiastical hierarchy, was widespread. There were many who would have agreed with William Lovett, the Chartist leader, that they had come 'to look upon practical Christianity as a union for the promotion of brotherly kindness and good deeds to one another, and not a thing of form and profession for the mercenary idlers to profit by'.[7] From this position it was but a short step to Deism or a general humanist philosophy. For those who could not stomach the claims of the churches, George Jacob Holyoake in the 1840s provided the religion of secularism. Early Victorian Britain was the scene of many spectacular losses of religious faith in the literary world, of which George Eliot, James Anthony Froude, and Francis Newman are the best-known examples; and among working class reformers a strong anticlerical and Paineite tradition was preserved. Yet the ethical standards of unbelievers were the same as those of professed Christians. Their morality was as puritanical as that of strict church or chapel goers. They were models of rectitude in their devotion to duty. To this code of belief and ethics, followed by Christians and unbelievers alike, we may give the name evangelicalism. In the previous generation the Evangelicals had been a group of devout, Calvinist-minded reformers within the Anglican Church. But for the Victorians the values with which the Evangelicals were associated became an orthodoxy, and evangelicalism (Christian or secular) part of the ideology of the age. Carlyle, writing in the *Westminster Review* of February 1838, commented with his usual perspicacity that the age was 'destitute of faith and yet terrified at scepticism'.

When we say, then, that the early Victorian period was a religious age we do not mean that everyone went to church (though a large proportion of the population in fact did so) but that Protestant evangelicalism was a basic ingredient in the dominant ideology. Men's values and standards, their assumptions and attitudes, functioned within this context. Religion as a social force operated at a number of different levels. For the middle classes, evangelical fervour could find an outlet either in a philanthropy calculated to mitigate, without changing the social basis of the evils of industrial society, or in schemes for radical social reform. Among the working classes religion could be at once a consolation and social sedative, or an inspiration in the struggle for social justice. The exact blending of these conflicting social attitudes depended upon local and personal factors in church and chapel. A Dr Hook or a William Thornton exercised a social no less than a religious leadership; and it was from the pulpit, whether in church or camp meeting, that public opinion was largely educated. In this broad sense, the churches and chapels were social educators, helping to mould and unify the atomistic elements of early nineteenth century society into a series of small communities.

Mental and Moral Improvement

The most spectacular problems of the new industrial age were the material ones. It was the squalid cellar dwellings, the open drains, and the utter poverty and destitution exposed by the probings of social investigators which roused the middle class conscience in the 1840s. Yet ultimately these were not the most intractable of the problems of the new society. In time the housing was improved, the streets were paved and sewered, and here and there a little of Victorian prosperity trickled down to the working classes. The physical problems, enormous as they seemed to sensitive contemporaries, could be solved, given the necessary time and money and will. The intangible problems of human relations were far more baffling. In the new towns of the industrial North had emerged a totally new type of community, in which the old techniques of social living had broken down. The new society was torn by the conflicts of attitudes and interests which marked the disintegration of a traditional culture and the emergence of a wider, technical civilisation. A great poverty of social life at all levels marked the new town; and a process of social disintegration paralleled the physical break-up of the town into a series of concentric circles of suburbs based on social distinction. The initiative in the solution of these problems lay with the middle classes, and their answer was to make over the whole of society in their own image. The ideas and standards and methods which had brought them such conspicuous success could do the same for all the people – if only they would let them. 'What some men are,' declared Samuel Smiles in *Self-Help*, 'all without difficulty might be. Employ the same means, and the same results will follow.'

The popular slogan for this much-desired transformation was Improvement. Indeed, so widely used was the term that historians have labelled the early and mid Victorian periods the Age of Improvement. Many meanings were put upon the word improvement: sometimes it was used simply as a synonym for change in general, or for progress. But frequently it was used with the adjectives mental or moral, and then it referred to changes in values. One of the social effects of evangelicalism was to internalise the puritan values of hard work and self-reliance, and inculcate a strong sense of duty. To spread these values beyond the middle classes and skilled artisans to the labouring population at large was the object of most schemes for mental and moral improvement in the 1830s and 1840s. The overall aim was the strengthening of a common culture, based on middle class social norms, into which the working classes could be integrated. Respectability was the goal to be striven for, and self-improvement the way to attain it.

Early industrial society, to a far greater extent than any previous age, was based on the written word. The socialising functions of print were fully realised, and the 'whip of the word' was a most powerful agent in shaping the new society. Print served to destroy traditional attitudes to work and substitute new norms and goals. The work patterns of an older, semi-rural population were unsuited to the needs of a factory age. Habits of Saint Monday (when artisans absented themselves from work on Monday to recover from the excesses of the weekend) had to be replaced by the discipline of a regular and reliable force of mill hands. This was not an easy task, nor was it accomplished in one generation. Coercion had to be applied in various forms, from strict factory rules to the inculcation of precepts of self-discipline. The latter was in the long run much the more effective, for it gave a man an inner guide as to what he ought to do and what he ought to be like. In the words of the American sociologist, David Riesman, it changed him from a tradition-directed to an inner-directed person.

The task to be accomplished was twofold: to break down the old and spread the new. The working classes had to be convinced that if only they would adapt themselves as rapidly as possible to the *status quo* they would benefit to the full in that 'good time coming' which was just round the corner. Traditional social habits and customs seldom fitted into the new pattern of industrial life, and they had therefore to be discredited as hindrances to progress. In the manufacturing towns a large working class population, with its roots in the popular culture of the countryside effectively severed, and disciplined to the routine of mill life, gradually acclimatised itself to the new ethos. After 1840 Sunday school processions and temperance teas began to replace traditional enjoyments of wrestling, cock-fighting and bull-baiting. Other holiday observances, such as rush-bearing, declined in the large industrial towns of the North, and railway excursions decreased workers' dependence on local forms of entertainment. Most middle class efforts to promote the mental and moral improvement of the labouring poor (whether through education, temperance or 'rational recreation') were in essence attempts to help the working classes to assimilate themselves more completely into the new society and to accept its values.

The process of assimilation was closely related to the spread of literacy. That fairly widespread illiteracy amongst the working classes existed in early Victorian England and Wales, despite a considerable amount of voluntary educational effort of various kinds, is clear from the statistics of the marriage registers (where brides and grooms who could not write their names signed with a X). Joseph Brook, a weaver who gave evidence before the Assistant Handloom Weavers' Commission in 1839, estimated that two-thirds of the adult weavers in Bradford could read but that not above a quarter could write. In general the figures for the 1840s show that about two-thirds of the male population and half of the female were literate, at any rate to the extent of signing their names. But there were considerable regional differences in literacy rates which are not very easy to explain. After 1840 the percentage of literate persons increased, although for some time there was also an absolute increase in illiterates because of the growth in population. The root cause of illiteracy was inadequate elementary education. In 1851 there were nearly five million children of school age, that is, between three and fifteen. Of these, 600,000 were at work, over two million were in school, and the remainder were neither at work nor school.

The institutions of education were a strange assortment of ancient privilege and recent innovation. For the aristocracy, gentry and wealthy middle classes the Public Schools provided an education for leadership, which successfully integrated the old and new wealth into a ruling élite. In the cities and market towns the old grammar schools offered a traditional, classics-based curriculum for the sons of local tradesmen and businessmen. For the children of the labouring classes three main types of institution existed: the private day school (including the dame school), the Sunday school, and the factory school. The great majority of working class pupils in common day schools were under the age of ten, and many attended for only two or three years. The quality of education in such schools was low, for the teachers were un-qualified and the charge per head (school pence) was under 6d per week. Dame schools, intended for the youngest children, were usually little more than baby-minding establishments. Factory schools, established under the educational clauses of the 1833 Factories Act, were not much better than the private day schools. The Sunday schools, which had grown rapidly since their foundation in the 1780s, were handicapped by the part-time basis of their operation, and were perhaps mainly useful in giving able boys a start from which they could go on to educate them-selves. Even when the school pence were forthcoming and parents were willing and able to forgo their children's earnings for some years, the restricted curricula and haphazard organisation of primary education were such as to provide at best a certain amount of 'instruction' and seldom a genuine education. With limited facilities for primary education the educational aspirations of the working classes tended to be kept low.

The existence of perhaps a quarter or a third of the labouring poor who were totally illiterate, and a further percentage whose literacy was only rudimentary, constituted a barrier to the spread of middle class ideology. An increase in the provision of element-ary school facilities was the main response to this challenge. Encouraged by a modest annual grant of £20,000 from the gov-ernment in 1833 (increased to £30,000 in 1839) and by the set-ting up of a small central administration and inspectorate, the voluntary religious school societies built a network of elementary schools across the country. Thanks to the religious rivalry between the two main providing bodies – the British and Foreign School Society and the National Society – a system of public elementary education was established. The creation of a fully literate society was an imperative in the dominant philosophies of the age. Evangelicalism and utilitarianism put a premium on a minimum of literary facility. An illiterate man could be a good Christian, but it was a definite advantage if he could read the scriptures. Even more did the utilitarians require a literary basis for society. A rational appeal could doubtless be comprehended by an intelligent though unlettered artisan, but the process of communication was all but defeated without the medium of the written word. So well was this understood by Henry Brougham and his radical-Whig followers that they were justly dubbed by John Henry Newman (the leader of the Oxford movement) 'the knowledge school'. Their monuments were the mechanics' institutes and the Society for the Diffusion of Useful Knowledge.

Formal schooling was not the only means to the creation of a literate society, in which a regard for knowledge and print were the hallmark of working class respectability. It was Gibbon who observed that every man who rises above the common level has received two educations: the first from other people, the second and more important, from himself. The Victorians took this greatly to heart. 'Be assured, brother mechanic, there's nothing like observing, and thinking, and doing things for oneself,' counselled the self-educated Timothy Claxton.[8] Encouragement to educational self-help found willing acceptance by many intelligent working men, for it harmonised with an older and indigenous minority tradition of exceptional artisans who were prepared to pay almost any price to educate themselves in the fullest sense of the term. When a fluent reader of the daily newspaper was wont to be thought a 'great scholar' and 'a far-learned man',[9] the influence and prestige of self-educated working men among their class gave them a social importance out of all proportion to their numbers. They provided the only indigenous leadership for the people in religious, social-reform and political movements. At the same time they were a point of contact with middle class ideals – a dual role which sometimes created a dangerous ambiguity. In some areas, such as the West Riding of Yorkshire, this tradition was particularly strong, and it was frequently connected with certain trades, notably shoemaking and weaving. Some of these self-cultured artisans continued to ply their old trades all their lives, so that they became known as 'So and So, the Weaver-Poet'; others, dissatisfied with their previous life, turned to journalism, political reform, and the Methodist ministry. But whatever their choice they represented a distinctive element, found in varying degrees of intensity, and combined with various interests and movements, in working class life in early Victorian Britain. The famous names of self-educated working class leaders, such as William Cobbett, Samuel Bamford, William Lovett, and Thomas Cooper lived long in popular memory, perpetuated in rough-framed prints on cottage walls, in oral traditions of reform and Chartist meetings, and in their autobiographies.

The institutions of mental improvement were usually simple and unpretentious, reflecting directly what working men felt to be their needs. Typical of this tradition was the mutual improvement society, consisting of a small number of members who met together either in each other's houses or in a small room hired for the purpose. A few simple rules, a programme of classes, essay readings, and discussions were drawn up, and a small stock of books was collected as the basis of a little library. The instruction was given voluntarily by the members themselves, and was designed primarily to promote proficiency in the three Rs; but in some instances was extended to geography, history, French and chemistry. A discussion circle and opportunities for practising public speaking in debates were also frequently provided. The very simplicity of these societies was their chief virtue, providing a seed which could germinate rapidly in many different kinds of soil. 'They may be regarded,' wrote Smiles, 'as the Educational Methodism of our day.'[10]

It was in such an environment that the most famous self-improvement manual of the day, Samuel Smiles' *Self-Help*, had its origin. In 1844 four young men in Leeds started a mutual improvement society, and they were soon joined by other operatives. They met at first in a room of a cottage of one of the members; but when summer came they migrated to an old garden house, where, amidst rakes and hoes and broken flowerpots, they taught themselves reading, writing, grammar and arithmetic. When winter came round again they hired a room which had been used as a temporary cholera hospital, and which for that reason they obtained cheaply as no one else would risk using it. By March 1845 their numbers had grown to about a hundred, and 'growing ambitious, they desired to have lectures delivered to them'.[11] At this point Smiles, who was practising as a physician in Leeds, got to know them, for they invited him 'to talk to them a bit'. He was touched by their 'admirable self-helping spirit', and accordingly addressed them several times on the theme of men who had risen from poverty and obscurity by their own efforts. From these lectures came the nucleus of *Self-Help*, which sold a quarter of a million copies during its author's lifetime and which was translated into all the chief languages of Europe and Asia. The book was not published until 1859, and its direct influence therefore lies outside the early Victorian era. But in origin it was a product of the 1840s.

Smiles claimed no originality for *Self-Help*. Indeed, he did no more than restate in an attractive form a doctrine that had already begun to appear elsewhere. Periodicals such as the *Penny Magazine* (edited by Charles Knight for the Society for the Diffusion of Useful Knowledge) and *Chambers's Edinburgh Journal* had from 1832 printed many 'instructive' and 'improving' articles. Educational self-help had been advocated in little manuals like George L. Craik's *The Pursuit of Knowledge under Difficulties* (1830); and from 1848–52 the literature of improvement swelled the pages of magazines such as the *Family Economist* and the *Family Friend*. Advice on self-improvement was not confined to working men: in many ways it was even more attractive to lower middle class clerks and shop assistants. Improvement was the key to success in life, the secret of how to get on. Accordingly, books of advice to 'young men of the lower orders', to women, to servants and apprentices, to businessmen, were produced. Often they had a definitely religious starting point, as in the case of the YMCA series of *Lectures to Young Men* (1849–50). Two dominant themes ran through all this advice: the gospel of work and the doctrine of self-help.

It was widely agreed that the foremost quality necessary for success in life was industry, the capacity and willingness for hard work. This, not genius, was the secret of most successful men. 'The qualities necessary to ensure success,' Smiles assured his readers, 'are not at all extraordinary. They may, for the most part, be summed up in these two – common sense and perseverance.'[11] The latter was indispensably linked with application: no legend was more popular than King Robert the Bruce and the spider. Such effort was necessary in the first place to earn a socially adequate income; and such an income was the basis of independence, without which a man could not be considered free. In relation to this central aim of independence, the lesser virtues of frugality, self-denial, and thrift stood as means to an end. Thrift appeared to Smiles as an effective agency for working class betterment precisely because it would make the working man independent; it would enable him to become a truly free man instead of a wage slave. The power of a penny a day saved, he argued, was potentially a greater force for working class emancipation than Chartism, universal suffrage, or strikes.

Besides thrift there were numerous ancillary aids to success. Punctuality and early rising were essential in young people. So also were habits of orderliness – for just as genius seldom dispensed with the need for hard work, so success was seldom attained by accident. Leisure was not to be wasted but used. 'One of the hours each day wasted on trifles or indolence, is enough to make an ignorant man wise in ten years', claimed a writer in the *Family Friend*. A concern for the little things in life was not to be despised; positively because if one takes care of the pence the pounds take care of themselves, and negatively because a little sin leads to a big one. More important still was a 'prudent' marriage in accordance with Malthusian precepts. 'Marriage without means is like a horse without beans', repeated the manuals on happy homes; and 'Before you marry be sure of a home wherein to tarry', advised the writers of moral stories in the family magazines. There were also other desirable, though not strictly essential ingredients. Piety and religious observance, adherence to temperance principles, and avoidance of bad temper had obvious material value. Conversely, 'sensual' amusements, religious infidelity, trade disputes, and political agitation were to be avoided.

The full fruits of this teaching were not reaped by the early Victorians but by the succeeding two generations. Nevertheless the basic tenets of this social ethic were abundantly clear by the 1840s. Contemporaries felt that the combination of certain moral qualities with a few simple techniques of living would produce those habits most conducive to success. The pedigree of these ideas of social morality was puritan, transmitted through the dominant evangelicalism of the middle and respectable working classes. It was thus that the social devices and conveniences of the age acquired the compulsion of moral, even religious virtues. They were popularised in many forms, but particularly as proverbs and aphorisms. *Self-Help* was full of them; the *Family Economist* from 1848 to 1851 printed them as a border round its cover; and Martin Tupper used them as the basis of his enormously popular *Proverbial Philosophy* (First series, 1838). To argue that 'Satan finds mischief for idle hands', or 'Where there's a will there's a way', was to present a middle class social outlook as the wisdom of the ages. It put the weight of tradition and common sense behind social values and interpretations which were in reality peculiar to one particular age.

Self-help in the 1840s appeared to be a means whereby the working classes might secure some measure of personal and social advance. Later middle class enthusiasm for the virtues of self-help integrated it into the dominant philosophy of individualism, emphasising its value as a means of strengthening independent citizenship as opposed to ideas of collective or communal responsibility for social ills. But in its original expression, as a spontaneous response to working class needs, self-help frequently assumed a collective form. The mutual improvement society, the friendly benefit society, the cooperative store and the trade union were organisations set up by working men to do together something which they could not do so well alone. Smiles at the time when he first became interested in mutual improvement societies was sympathetic to collectivist and cooperative ideas, and had only recently relinquished the editorship of the radical *Leeds Times*. Subsequently the doctrine of self-help underwent a transformation, and what had been originally a working class device to try to grasp some of those cultural and material benefits which were denied them in the new industrial society, became the middle class reply to workers' demands for better social conditions. Once state action in social and economic affairs was ruled out of court, some alternative path to social betterment had to be offered to the working classes. This was provided, along with other remedies such as moral restraint, in the philosophy of self-help. It provided a positive side to *laissez-faire*, applicable in the educational, social and economic fields alike. Moreover, self-help had the advantage of being not only a practical social programme but also a moral virtue; if the labouring classes were poor and ignorant it was, in the ultimate analysis, because they were morally deficient. 'There is no reason,' wrote Smiles in *Self-Help*, 'why the condition of the average workman in this country should not be a useful, honourable, respectable and happy one'; self-help, which had already raised some working men, could do the same for all.

The social reality, however, was far different from this comfortable ideology. It was clear to many middle class sympathisers before 1850 that self-help as a means of raising the labouring classes as a whole had severe limitations. A minority of exceptional working men could be relied on to respond to such opportunities; but for vast numbers of the labouring poor the suggestion of self-help was simply advice to lift themselves by their own bootstraps. The minimum requirement was for some initial assistance from the middle classes; though even that could not surmount the common obstacle among the poorest of the working classes of complete indifference or hostility to the advantages of self-help. Like the millions who were absent from church on census Sunday, the large number of labouring men unaffected by ideals of self-improvement worried contemporaries. It is clear from such evidence as Mayhew's that, despite all the evangelical effort that was poured out, decade after decade, considerable sections of the labouring poor, especially in large cities, were culturally resistant to the dominant values of respectable Victorian society. Not until long after mid century were these resistances modified or broken down.

In the meantime the early Victorians were not without encouragement that in some areas at least their efforts seemed eminently successful. The Great Exhibition of 1851 was a symbol of the ideals and achievements of the early Victorians. It was in every way an enormous success, far exceeding the fondest hopes of its promoters (led by the Prince Consort) and completely disproving the early fears and criticisms voiced in *The Times*. Designed by Joseph Paxton (who had previously built a great conservatory at Chatsworth for his patron, the Duke of Devonshire), the huge building of glass and iron in Hyde Park captured the imagination of the nation. Over six million people visited the Crystal Palace (as *Punch* so aptly christened the building) and a handsome profit was made. The 100,000 exhibits covered every imaginable aspect of mid nineteenth century civilisation; and though ingenuity and extravagance were perhaps more in evidence than good taste, the 'visibility of progress' was plain for all to see. Especially was the exhibition a triumph of British industrial superiority; for despite the title of 'Great Exhibition of the Works of Industry of all Nations', over half the exhibitors were from Britain and the empire, and the whole enterprise was intended to impress foreigners with the British way of life. Bizarre as were some of the exhibits (a collapsible piano for gentlemen's yachts, a knife with three hundred blades, Gothic furniture in cast bronze), the popular machinery court left no doubt as to the reality of technical achievement.

The themes of the Great Exhibition were intended to be as much moral as material. To honour the gospel of work and the Smilesian virtues was a main object of the venture, and there was much reference to 'the working bees of the world's hive'. The theme of international peace was also repeatedly emphasised; and the exhibition was taken as a demonstration of the way in which commerce and free trade would promote friendship and cooperation between nations. Religiosity was much to the fore. At the opening ceremony the Archbishop of Canterbury invoked God's blessing upon the enterprise. After giving thanks that 'violence is not heard in our land, wasting nor destruction within its borders', he warned his hearers against hubris:

Whilst we survey the works of art and industry which surround us, let not our hearts be lifted up that we forget the Lord our God, as if our own power or the might of our own hands had gotten us this wealth. . . . Both riches and honour come of Thee, and Thou reignest over all.[12]

Following this 'short and appropriate prayer' (as the Queen recorded in her journal), the choirs burst forth in the Hallelujah chorus.

6
Social Change and Social Movements

Despite the reassuring tones of the Archbishop's remarks at the Great Exhibition, the 'visibility of progress' was not without its more worrying side. The magnificent technical achievements had been bought only at the price of vast economic and social upheaval. The pace of change in the previous twenty-five years had been unequalled in human history hitherto, and this was the main concern of all reflective commentators of the time. They were aware that in many areas of national life the tight grip of tradition had been largely broken, and that 'ancient wisdom' in matters of belief, values, and social relationships was being increasingly questioned. Progress, improvement, reform – all implied change; and change meant that the equilibrium of society was to a greater or lesser extent upset. Today most advanced Western societies have come to take account of this situation, and have developed approved patterns of change and innovation, though they have not been able to eliminate strains and conflicts entirely. In early Victorian Britain the strains and tensions of adjustment were very great, and the fear of a complete breakdown resulting in revolution, as in France, haunted contemporaries (who could fully share the Archbishop's thankfulness that 'violence is not heard in our land').

As we saw in earlier chapters, the stability of British society in the 1830s and 1840s was based on a network of institutions which maintained the dominance of an élite and the subordination of the lower orders. Habits of deference, hierarchical assumptions, and an ideology which made acceptance of the social system seem 'natural', constituted an effective form of social control. The system however was not closed or rigid. Certain types of change were possible and permissible within the system; and in certain contexts the system itself, or important parts of it, could be changed. In this chapter we shall look a little more closely at some of the ways in which social change could be brought about, first by the movement of individuals, and then by the collective pressure of organised social movements.

Social mobility, or the movement of individuals within a society, can be considered in at least four different ways.[1] First, there is the phenomenon of geographical mobility, or the movement of population from one part of the country to another. Of this order was the migration to the manufacturing and business centres from the surrounding counties, and the great Irish immigration which swelled massively after the famine of 1846–7. In many northern industrial towns the population contained a high proportion of first-generation immigrants, which complicated the social problems of urbanisation. Bradford's population in 1841 contained over 10 per cent of immigrants from outside Yorkshire: in 1851 the proportion was over 20 per cent. Spatial mobility on this scale was something quite new and distinctive. Traditionally society had always sought to reduce movement to a minimum by devices such as the Settlement Acts, designed to prevent labourers from migrating to (and gaining a 'settlement' in) another parish, where they might become eligible for poor relief; but by the 1840s effective restrictions on migration had broken down in many areas. Historians have not yet examined fully the implications of this type of movement from one community to another. It seems likely, however, that problems of social integration or isolation are relevant to such questions as the development of class consciousness, forms of popular social action, and varieties of working class culture.

The second dimension of social mobility, that of occupational change, has received a little more attention, though hard data is extremely scarce. We have noted earlier the degree of movement between the upper middle classes and the gentry and aristocracy, and also within the ranks of the middle classes themselves.

Lower down the scale the barriers between manual and non-manual jobs and between the skilled artisan and the labourer restricted mobility, though they did not entirely prevent it. Indeed, the ideology of self-help held out the promise of upward mobility as a reward for hard work and sober living. To the extent that there was a gap between the promises of mobility and the social situation of the labouring poor, self-help was a myth. But myths can play an important role in motivating social action, and we do not at present know how widely the ideology of mobility was believed in.

An interesting piece of evidence comes from Bradford. John V. Godwin, a leading member of the local mechanics' institute and a stuff merchant in the town, read a paper on the institute before the annual meeting of the Social Science Association in 1859.[2] Addressing himself to the question of what benefit the working classes had derived from the Bradford Mechanics' Institute, he stated that:

> Those who have watched the Bradford Mechanics' Institute are able to state that they have seen year after year, an unbroken stream of youths, sons of working men, rising to positions of responsibility, which in all probability they never would have filled without its aid, and in many cases entering upon and pursuing a successful middle class career by the habits, the knowledge, and the connections acquired in this Institute. Striking instances will occur to those acquainted with the facts, any of which it would be invidious to name.

To substantiate this claim he then quoted details of the members of the writing and arithmetic class, which in 1842 consisted of forty members, with an average attendance of twenty-six. Some of these were now dead; but in the case of twenty-six of the members it was possible to give their father's occupation in 1842 and their own occupation both in 1842 and 1859. The statistics were as follows:

Father's occupation in 1842 – Unknown, 6; woolsorters, 6; wool-combers, 5; plasterer, 1; sawyer, 1; overlookers, 3; weaver, 1; middle class, 3.

Son's occupation in 1842 – In offices, 3; woolcomber, 1; factory boys,

4; shop boy, 1; in warehouses, 10; apprenticed to mechanics, 3; shoemaker, 1; printer, 1; joiner, 1; bookbinder, 1.

Present position – Working classes, 1; in responsible positions as book-keepers, clerks, schoolmasters, commercial travellers, wool buyers, and salesmen, 16; successful men of business, and some of them highly so, 9.

And to further strengthen his case, he added:

Remarkable as this result is, I can only say that the year has been selected, not as one of the most favourable, but solely because it is the most remote of which any such record is kept, and therefore there is less probability of trespassing on individual feeling.

This of course was mobility from the working to the middle classes. It does not tell us anything about occupational advance within the working classes, say from unskilled labourer's son to the ranks of the aristocracy of labour.

A third aspect of social mobility is the acquirement of property, real and personal. In the case of movement into the gentry from business or industry, the purchase of a landed estate was crucial. For the middle classes, home-ownership was the test. It is clear, for example, from the middle class arguments supporting schemes for artisans to purchase their cottages through savings and build-ing societies, that such property ownership was regarded as a social step upwards. Among the mass of labouring people who could never hope to save enough to buy their home, the possession of personal property was an important determinant of social position. The acquirement of carpets, mahogany furniture and ornaments represented an advance in social status as well as in comfort. The development of that peculiar Victorian arrangement, the parlour (a sort of domestic shrine in which the most treasured household goods were displayed but seldom used), was the logical and later outcome of this attitude.

Lastly, we may distinguish a fourth type of social mobility, the cultural and religious. By adopting new cultural habits, especially those of the class above them, men were able to assist their social movement upwards. This was very clear in the case of the mechanics' institutes which had been originally founded to provide opportunities for the study of science by artisans, but which from the mid-1830s catered mainly to the needs of the lower middle classes. Changes in the curricula and methods of study in the institutes were made to accommodate the new clientèle of clerks and shopkeepers, who wanted not science and the discipline of study, but the opportunity to acquire a little of the cultural elegance which they noted in their social superiors. Instead of classes in chemistry and mathematics, the mechanics' institutes by the 1840s were offering popular lectures, soirées and phrenology. Upward mobility was also assisted by changes in religious affiliation. It was frequently noted that as Wesleyan Methodists prospered they tended to become Anglicans. The various denominations differed in their social standing, with the Church of England at the top of the scale, the Old Dissent and the Wesleyans in the middle, and the smaller Protestant sects at the bottom. The Roman Catholics, who had grown rapidly in numbers with the Irish immigration, stood outside this social continuum, though most of their congregations were heavily working class. The switch from chapel to church attendance was a social signal that a family was moving up in the world. Between the Nonconformist bodies there was similar mobility, from Primitive Methodism, via the New Connexion to Wesleyanism; or from back-street meeting house to fashionable down-town chapel. The exact nature of the change was determined by the local religious ethos, and might take place over more than one generation. But whatever the details, the significant thing was that change in fact occurred; mobility in this, as in other aspects of social life, was a practicable possibility for a substantial number of people.

The patterns of change which we have so far considered were all approved by early Victorian society: they had become institutionalised, and some were sanctioned ideologically. But there were also pressures and organisations for change which were not socially approved and which could not so easily be accepted into the social system. They were directed towards changing parts of the social system itself, rather than securing changes for individuals within the system. Such developments are usually felt to be radical and dangerous, since they call into question certain fundamental beliefs and institutions of society. They pose a threat to the established order and demonstrate that the usual methods of maintaining social discipline are no longer effective. Fears are aroused, security seems threatened, and society reacts strongly to reassert 'law and order'. The advocates of change, faced with indifference or refusal to accept their demands, have either to back down or step up the pressure of their campaign. In the last resort they may appeal to force and attempt to gain their ends by armed revolution, or by the threat of it. At times of profound social and economic dislocation the chances of change by force and violence are increased. With widespread and deeply-felt economic grievances, an effective leadership and organisation of the popular cause, and a loss of nerve by the ruling élite, a revolutionary situation can develop. Not all of these factors were present in early Victorian Britain; but sufficient of them were there to arouse revolutionary hopes on the one hand and panic fears on the other.

No period in British history has been richer in movements for radical and social reform than the decades 1830–50. The list of only the major movements which flourished in these twenty years is an initial indication of the variety and extent of the efforts to bring about far-reaching changes in British society: political reform, Chartism, trade unionism, factory reform, Owenite socialism, cooperation, anti-Poor Law agitation, secularism, the struggle for an unstamped press, friendly benefit societies, workers' and adult education, temperance, phrenology, vegetarianism, universal peace, the Anti-Corn Law League, anti-state church campaign, millenarianism, machine-breaking and agricultural riots. The very existence of this plethora of movements suggests a general discontent on the part of many people with their lot under the new conditions of industrialism and a determination to try to change things.

It is not easy to construct a typology of these movements. Contemporary reformers were confused by the legion of causes and sought a reconciliation in the idea of universal or general reform. They believed that between all reformers there was a sense of fellowship based on a common faith in reform as a law of nature. Particular reforms were of less importance than recognition of the universal duty to strive for social and individual betterment. As Joseph Barker put it, although we are all 'reformers of different stamps', we shall all 'contribute to one great end – the illumination and salvation of our race'.[3] Historians, faced with the need to examine the dynamics of social movements more analytically, have generally used concepts of class or social psychology to try to account for the different types of endeavour. In the remainder of this chapter we shall refer to some of these movements in more detail and suggest how and why they came to be such a characteristic part of the early Victorian scene.

Overshadowing all movements for change was reform, meaning political reform. In 1832, after fifty years of proposals, disappointments and agitation, the worst abuses and anomalies of the old parliamentary system were swept away. The franchise was extended to some of the urban middle classes (£10 householders) and the £50 tenant farmers in the counties, and there was a modest reorganisation of constituency representation. The Reform Bill was a party measure, carried by one section of the ruling élite (the Whigs) against the other (the Tories), amidst a great popular agitation throughout the country. For several months in 1831–2 the whole nation was in a turmoil; riots broke out in several towns and there was talk of armed insurrection. In the event the Reform Act proved to be a symbol rather than a substantive change: not until many years later were the bases of political power significantly altered. But reform as an idea had triumphed. Its opponents (the Duke of Wellington and the Tory Party) were discredited, and the initiative was now with the moderate reformers. It strengthened belief in the possibility and desirability of change. If Old Corruption (as Cobbett called the political power structure) could be successfully attacked, there was hope that other traditional institutions could be abolished or greatly modified. The Tories warned that reform would open the flood gates to many other forms of change. They were right,

though not in the catastrophic sense they feared. Reform became
the banner slogan of the age.

A combination of disillusionment with the Reform Act of
1832 and a continuing belief in the possibility and efficacy of
reform provided the immediate enthusiasm for the greatest of all
the popular movements, Chartism. Despite the Reform Act,
claimed a Chartist pamphlet of 1836, out of six million males of
voting age only 840,000 have the franchise, and one-fifth of the
latter elect a majority of the House of Commons; which means
that one-fortieth of the adult male population has the power to
make laws binding on all the rest. For nearly twenty years after
1837, Chartism was a name to evoke the wildest hopes and the
worst fears, like Bolshevism in a later age. Some historians have
seen Chartism as a forerunner of the Labour Party and the modern
labour movement, which in a sense it was. Certainly no other
movement before the rise of modern labour and socialism at the
end of the century had anything like the mass following of
Chartism. It was the first attempt to build an independent political
party representing the interests of the labouring and unprivileged
sections of the nation. But we should be careful not to press these
parallels too far, lest we fall into the common error of reading
into the past the experiences and assumptions of the present. After
all, the society in which the Chartists had to operate was very
different from Britain fifty years later; and in fact the direct links
between Chartism and the modern labour movement are extremely tenuous. If we are content to accept Chartism for what
it was to the men of the 1830s, and seek to interpret it in the
context of early Victorian society, we shall avoid some of the
difficulties that later writers have experienced. For example,
contemporaries noted that for many of its followers Chartism
was basically 'a knife and fork question'. Yet its programme was a
series of political demands. This has puzzled historians, who have
concluded that one of the main reasons for Chartism's lack of
success was its contradiction in seeking political remedies for
economic grievances. In fact the Chartists' tactics made a good
deal of sense at that time, and their analysis of what we should
now call the power structure was evidently shrewder than the

historians'. The link between economic ills and political representation was constantly elaborated in Chartist pamphlets and oratory; how, it was asked, could a 'rotten House of Commons', representing the interests of landholders, speculators, manufacturers and capitalists, be expected to do anything but uphold an economic system in which the poor were ground down and oppressed? Given the options open to them in the 1830s, and the experience of alternative paths which they had pursued and found blocked, the Chartists' programme for social advance through political power was perfectly sound. It was also the method adopted, though with more success, by the middle classes; and this lesson was by no means lost upon the Chartists. If Chartism did not gain its objectives, the reasons have to be sought elsewhere than in the apparent paradox of economic ends through political means. It is also salutary to remember that movements which 'failed' did not necessarily have to fail. History is not simply a record of success stories.

The Chartists were so named because they formulated their demands in a six point charter: universal (manhood) suffrage, annual parliaments, vote by (secret) ballot, abolition of the property qualification for MPs, payment of MPs, and equal electoral districts. The object was to make the charter the law of the land, by legal, constitutional means if possible, or by force if necessary – or by a mixture of both. Most Chartist leaders were reluctant to be labelled as 'moral force' or 'physical force' men. 'We will have the charter,' they declared, 'peaceably if we can, forcibly if we must.' Great efforts were made to collect support for a petition to the House of Commons on behalf of the charter; but on each occasion that it was presented the House rejected its demands. Alternative methods were therefore bound to be advocated. There were plans for making the central body of Chartist delegates, the national convention, a people's parliament to bypass Westminster; a general strike ('national holiday') was attempted in August 1839; and local riots, and perhaps an abortive insurrection (in November, 1839), showed that physical force might not be ruled out. But the Chartists were unable to repeat the tactics of 1830–2, when the Reform Bill was carried by a combination of support in Parliament and the threat of force outside.

There was little that was new in the six points of the charter. They were drawn up by William Lovett and his friends in the London Working Men's Association in 1837, though the People's Charter was not officially published until the following year. Politically Chartism was in the central tradition of British radicalism, stretching back to the Corresponding Societies of 1792–3, and the Chartists were proud of their heritage. It was a tradition of mass meetings, imprisonments and conflicts with authority. In the provinces Working Men's Associations were formed on the London model in 1837, in each case building on the remains of earlier radical reform organisations, such as the Political Unions which had carried on the popular struggle for the Reform Bill. The earlier martyrs of the radical cause were constantly remembered in Chartist speeches, and no rally was complete without a banner commemorating the 'Massacre of Peterloo' at Manchester in 1819.

The origins of Chartism, however, were more complex than a simple development from the London Working Men's Association. In Birmingham the movement at first was closely allied with middle class radicals and currency reformers. In Leeds, Owenite socialists combined with middle class radicals and physical force militants to launch the Leeds Working Men's Association. And in other towns of the West Riding and the industrial North and North-east local movements and grievances provided a basis for Chartism. Thus right from the start Chartism was not a national movement with its central headquarters in London, but a series of local and regional movements loosely federated together. This posed a problem of concerted action which was never solved. Attempts to build a national organisation repeatedly fell apart; and the most effective link between Chartists was not their system of delegates to a national convention, but the widely-read Chartist newspaper, *The Northern Star*. The geography of Chartism highlights a characteristic which is found in other contemporary movements, such as the Anti-Corn Law League, namely, the strength of provincial roots and the relative isolation of London. A clue to the reasons for this can be found in the economic and social patterns described in earlier chapters.

The point has been made that the British economy in the period 1830-50 was only partly industrialised, and that machinery and factory organisation had been introduced unevenly between different industries and between different sectors of the same industry. Levels of wages, employment opportunities, social relationships, and general working conditions varied between industries and localities, creating different types and intensities of grievance. Within the labouring population divisions were created by differences of skill and earnings. Chartism was directly related to these varieties within the labour force, and faithfully reflected them in its regional peculiarities. Wherever there was a substantial number of skilled artisans, especially shoemakers, printers, tailors and cabinet makers, a Chartist organisation on the lines of the Working Men's Associations was to be expected, with an emphasis on self-help, independence, and propaganda for universal suffrage. Such was the movement in London or Birmingham. But in areas where there were substantial numbers of distressed handloom weavers, as in Lancashire and the West Riding, Chartism assumed an altogether fiercer visage and adopted a more strident tone. The idol of the Northern Chartists was not the reasoned, respectable artisan, William Lovett, with his appeal to 'the most intelligent and influential portion of the working classes', but the flamboyant Irish orator, Feargus O'Connor, who claimed to be the champion of the 'unshorn chins, blistered hands, and fustian jackets'. In Leicestershire and the East Midlands the backbone of the Chartist movement were the framework knitters – another group of domestic workers labouring, like the handloom weavers, in an over-stocked trade. There was a close correlation between the distribution of knitting frames and the strength of Chartism; Leicester, Loughborough and Hinckley were centres of the hosiery industry and also Chartist strongholds; in the eastern half of Leicestershire, where there were practically no frames, Chartism did not develop. Leeds and Sheffield in the 1840s produced another type of Chartism, based on lower middle class radicalism and artisan support. The Chartists in these towns elected their own candidates to the Town Council and concerned themselves with local issues of importance to shopkeepers and tradesmen.

Just as the local variations of Chartism were related to the structure of the economy, so the chronology of the movement reflected the cycle of booms and slumps between 1836 and 1851. The first climax of Chartism came in the winter of 1839, at the height of the trade depression. In 1842 a second peak of Chartist activity was reached with the Plug riots, arising out of mass unemployment in the Northern towns. And the last great flare-up of Chartism came in 1848, following a winter of economic recession and inspired by revolutions on the Continent. In periods of relative prosperity (1843–7 and after 1848) Chartism lost its mass support. It then became a movement promoting education, temperance, municipal reforms, and settlement on the land – while never losing faith that universal suffrage would some day, somehow, be won. After 1848, as a tantalising sort of epilogue, a group of Chartists tried to steer the movement towards social-ism and the international working class movement of Marx and Engels.

If, as has been stressed, Chartism was in many ways a logical development within the tradition of radical reform, in what sense was it a distinctive movement, and in what lay its significance as a vehicle for social change in the 1830s and 1840s? Two charac-teristics seem to stand out from the Chartist record, especially in its early phase; first, its class-conscious tone and temper; second, its mass size. There are not many points in modern British history at which the historian can profitably speculate whether a revolutionary situation might have developed but did not. Among the dates for consideration, however, would have to be included the winter of 1839 and the spring and summer of 1848. At both these times Chartism seemed, to many contem-poraries, to pose the threat of the barricades.

Chartists of many shades of opinion emphasised that their movement was concerned to promote the interests of working men as a class. The artisans of the Working Men's Associations no less than the distressed handworkers of the North assumed the need for class solidarity, and their leaders talked the language of class struggle. They denounced the Reform Act of 1832 as a middle class measure, complained that the working classes had been deliberately duped, and argued that Whigs and Tories alike were enemies of the people. An old Chartist writing at the end of the century commented:

People who have not shared in the hopes of the Chartists, who have no personal knowledge of the deep and intense feelings which animated them, can have little conception of the difference between our own times and those of fifty or sixty years ago. The whole governing classes – Whigs even more than Tories – were not only disliked, they were positively hated by the working population. Nor was this hostility to their own countrymen less manifest on the side of the 'better orders'.[4]

The picture of society here presented is very far from the comfortable, upper class ideal of stability and a modest degree of sanctioned change. By its appeal to smouldering social antagonisms and its articulation of class consciousness, Chartism struck at the roots of deference – which helps to account for the support it received from other non-deferential groups such as some members of the radical lower middle classes. So strong was the feeling of working class identification in Chartism that it defeated all attempts to form an alliance with middle class reformers in the Anti-Corn Law League or the Complete Suffrage Union. Even in Birmingham, where such an alliance had the greatest hope of success, the proposal to drop the name Charter in favour of some new organisation was sufficient to unite in opposition the mutually-antagonistic Chartist leaders, Lovett and O'Connor. When this working class consciousness was matched by an even stronger middle class consciousness, as was the case in the 1830s and 1840s, the possibility of social conflict was enhanced.

The fear of Chartism by the opulent classes was inspired by the very large number of followers who appeared to be sympathetic to its militant tactics. Membership of popular movements in the nineteenth century is difficult to assess, and accounts of numbers at meetings are notoriously divergent between one newspaper and another. Contemporaries, however, were agreed that attendances at Chartist meetings were greater than anything they could remember previously. Something of the tone of these rallies is conveyed by R. G. Gammage, the only Chartist to attempt a history of the movement. He is describing the torchlight meetings held on the Lancashire moors in the autumn of 1838:

for a short period the factory districts presented a series of such imposing popular demonstrations, as were perhaps never witnessed in any previous agitation. Bolton, Stockport, Ashton, Hyde, Staleybridge, Leigh, and various other places, large and small, were the scenes of these magnificent gatherings. At the whole of them the working people met in their thousands and tens of thousands to swear devotion to the common cause. It is almost impossible to imagine the excitement caused by these manifestations. . . . The people did not go singly to the place of meeting, but met in a body at a starting point, from whence, at a given time, they issued in huge numbers, formed into procession, traversing the principal streets, making the heavens echo with the thunder of their cheers on recognizing the idols of their worship in the men who were to address them, and sending forth volleys of the most hideous groans on passing the office of some hostile newspaper, or the house of some obnoxious magistrate or employer. The banners containing the more formidable devices, viewed by the red light of the glaring torches, presented a scene of awful grandeur. The death's heads represented on some of them grinned like ghostly spectres, and served to remind many a mammon-worshipper of his expected doom. The uncouth appearance of thousands of artizans who had not time from leaving the factory to go home and attend to the ordinary duties of cleanliness, and whose faces were therefore begrimed with sweat and dirt, added to the strange aspect of the scene. The processions were frequently of immense length, sometimes containing as many as fifty thousand people; and along the whole line there blazed a stream of light, illuminating the lofty sky, like the reflection from a large city in a general conflagration. The meetings themselves were of a still more terrific character. The very appearance of such a vast number of blazing torches only seemed more effectually to inflame the minds alike of speaker and hearers.[5]

Another, and less inflammatory type of Chartist meeting was the great open air rally held on a public holiday. Contingents would march, with bands and banners, from surrounding towns and villages to a central meeting place, where they would listen to speeches from local and national leaders. Booths and stalls were set up, and the marchers were accompanied by their sweethearts, wives and children, so that the whole gathering had some of the atmosphere of a fair. In the West Riding, for example, such Chartist rallies were held at Peep Green, a natural amphitheatre in the hills and equally accessible from all the main industrial towns of the region. Ben Wilson, the Halifax Chartist, estimated that 200,000 people were present at the meeting there on Whit Monday 1839.

Chartism made a deep impression on the labouring poor and assisted their transformation into a working class. The events of 1837–48 lived long in popular memory: the ghostly torchlight meetings, the skirmishes with police and troops, the drilling with pikes, the moulding of bullets in the cellar, arrest and imprisonment of local leaders, the escape to America when things got too hot at home – all served to add another chapter to the tradition of radical struggle. There was a strong romantic strain in all this: Chartist oratory and poetry was rich in denunciation of tyrants and proclamation of the glories of freedom; every imprisoned Chartist was portrayed as a noble martyr languishing in a dungeon. But the general result was a heightening of class awareness, a strengthening of the conviction that the working classes as such had special and separate interests, to which other classes were hostile or indifferent. The development of this class consciousness was an essential part of what E. P. Thompson has described as 'the making of the English working class'. At the same time Chartism was also rooted in an older and indigenous folk culture. It was a movement in the true sense of the word, and not just an organisation. Like other British reformers, the Chartists frequently appealed to ancient liberties, and presented their new demands as the restoration of traditional rights. While they called for class solidarity (or 'union of sentiment', as they put it), they also saw themselves as freeborn Englishmen.

In its most vigorous years (1837–42), Chartism seemed to swallow up lesser popular movements and to incorporate their demands with its own. The agitation against the New Poor Law in the North, which was extremely militant in 1837, was absorbed into the new Chartist movement – just as the Anti-Poor Law opposition had been led and supported by the stalwarts of the Short Time Committees, established in 1830–1 to work for factory reform. Contemporary with these movements was the struggle against the newspaper stamp duties, the 'taxes on knowledge'. Unstamped papers were published by radicals, who were then prosecuted and gaoled: between 1830 and 1836 over seven hundred people were prosecuted for selling unstamped papers, 219 of them in 1835. Trade union activity had increased rapidly after the repeal of the Combination Acts (declaring unions illegal) in 1824–5, and culminated in the Grand National Consolidated Trades Union which claimed to have a million members. In 1834 the employers moved against the new unionism, and the government made an example of the Tolpuddle Martyrs – six Dorsetshire labourers who were sentenced to seven years' transportation to Australia for administering an illegal oath in their newly formed trade union lodge. This severe check, soon to be followed by the economic recession of 1837–42, put an end to further union development until the return of prosperity in the 1840s. For the time being Chartism seemed to offer a better hope of advancement than trade unionism, and the new cause with the more urgent dynamic absorbed the energies of its predecessor. As movements faded into one another, a continuity was provided by the personnel. Many of the leaders, at both national and local level, were active in all these movements. A working man of radical inclinations did not limit himself to one particular cause, but rather supported all types of social and political agitation in the belief that they were all part of a general movement for change. Nor was there much exclusiveness in acquiring a social philosophy. Ideas from all sources were welcome, and eclecticism was no bar.

The most fruitful of these sources was Owenite socialism. Robert Owen, a successful industrialist who made a fortune in cotton spinning, elaborated his plans for social reconstruction in the years after the Napoleonic Wars. His first followers were mainly radical philanthropists, but in the late 1820s Owenism attracted support among working men. The trade union ferment of 1829–34 was dominated by Owenite theories, and for a few months in 1833–4 Owen was the acknowledged leader of the working classes. After the collapse of the Grand National Consolidated Trades Union, the Owenites developed a national organisation of agents and branches which carried on propaganda and social activities until about 1845. The institutions of Owenism, however, were never as influential as its social theories. Many working class leaders, who criticised Owen and the Owenites in the 1830s, nevertheless acknowledged their debt to Owenite socialism. Owenism provided a kind of reservoir from which different groups and individuals drew ideas and inspiration which they then applied as they chose.

Essentially Owenism was the main British variety of what Marx and Engels called utopian socialism, but which is more usefully described as communitarianism. The Owenites believed that society could be radically transformed by means of experimental communities, in which property was held in common and social and economic activity was organised on a cooperative basis. This was a method of effecting social change which was radical, peaceful and immediate. Between 1825 and 1847 seven Owenite communities were founded in Britain, the largest being at Orbiston in Scotland and East Tytherly, Hampshire. But attractive as the sectarian ideal of withdrawal from society in order to get on with building the 'new moral world' might appear in the grim years of the 1830s and 1840s, the communities did not flourish as had been hoped. Other Owenite institutions for changing society were scarcely more successful. Labour exchanges, where artisans could exchange the products of their labour through the medium of labour notes, did not spread beyond London and Birmingham. Only the cooperative trading stores, some of which were established by working men to accumulate funds for starting a community, proved eventually to be viable; and the continuous history of the modern cooperative movement is usually traced from the foundation of an Owenite store in Rochdale in 1844.

If Owenism did not produce strong and stable institutions,

it did provide a yeast of ideas which found their way into other movements. Communitarianism was a challenge to a society in which community values had been weakened by emphasis on individual enterprise, self-help and competition. The Owenites called themselves socialists from the mid-1830s because they wished to emphasise a social, as opposed to an individual, approach, in all fields of human endeavour, including economic organisation. They formulated a critique of capitalism and an alternative theory to orthodox political economy which were echoed by many working class leaders. The basis of the Owenite 'economy of cooperation' was a general labour theory of value, derived partly from a doctrine of natural right (as found in the works of John Locke) and partly from the economic arguments of the contemporary political economist, David Ricardo. If, as the Owenites maintained, labour is the source of all wealth, and men exchange their products according to the amount of labour embodied in them, it needed little theory to convince working men that they had a right to the whole produce of their labour – and, as a corollary, that if they were poor it must be because they were not receiving the full value of what they produced. No argument in the Owenite armoury was better calculated to appeal to working men than that which told them they were unjustly exploited. In the bargain between capital and labour, it was argued, labour received only a part of the wealth to which it was entitled. Further, competitive commercial society was fettered by inadequate demand; the depression of wages to subsistence level destroyed incentive to higher production by labouring men, and the low level of their consumption caused by inadequate purchasing power put a ceiling on production.

A favourite starting point for Owenite discussions was the contrast between 'wealth and misery' or the paradox of 'poverty in the midst of plenty'. Owen was one of the first men to realise the social significance of the great increase in productive power attained during the early years of the nineteenth century, and the potentiality of material abundance was fundamental to the Owenite case. Despite some elements of backward-looking agrarianism

and paternalism in the communities, Owenism did not turn its
back on the Industrial Revolution or try to take refuge in some
pre-machine idyll. Owen, as one of the most successful industrialists of his age, believed that for the first time in human history
the necessary material means were available to enable everyone
to lead a good life, free from poverty and insecurity. Yet in fact,
he argued, society suffered from 'the paralysing effects of super-
abundance', which he traced, in the short run, to machinery.
This was not inevitable, but was solely the result of the competitive system, and given a 'rational' arrangement of society,
machinery could be a blessing instead of a curse. In all Owenite
plans for community, machinery was posited as the basis for
reduced hours of labour and the elimination of heavy or disagreeable types of work. Under the competitive system, however,
machinery led to a devaluation of human labour; some men were
directly displaced by labour-saving machines, and the wages of
those remaining in work were forced down by the reservoir of
unemployed.

Other aspects of Owenism were also calculated to appeal to
men who rejected the orthodoxies of their time and were in
search of an alternative social philosophy. The gloom of Malthusianism was dispelled by Owen's conviction that productive
capacity (both industrial and agricultural) could rise faster than
population. And an unbounded optimism in the possibility of
social perfection was opened up by the Owenite doctrine that
individual and social character is overwhelmingly determined
by environment. The basic institutions of society – private
property, the family, religion – were all under attack from the
Owenites. They believed in some form of community of property
and social equality, and condemned all institutions that 'in-
dividualised' man. Owen saw the family as a main bastion of
private property and the guardian of all those qualities of individualism and self-interest to which he was opposed. The
fragmentation and disharmony which Owenites deplored in
competitive society they attributed largely to the institution of
the private family. Owen regarded the family as a fundamentally
divisive force, much more so than class. Hence he attacked the

family and refused to regard class divisions as primary. Closely associated with Owenite plans for familial reform were attacks on the marriage system, suggestions for divorce, and the advocacy of birth control. When to these was added a rejection of all religion, it is hardly surprising that Owenism seemed to its enemies to be a dangerously radical, immoral, and godless creed.

Yet paradoxically while Owenism repudiated the teachings of the orthodox Christian churches, it developed many of the characteristics of a millennial sect. Owen's vision of the new moral world became a secularised version of the millennium, and some of his closest followers were millennialists. At this point we are brought close to the 'underworld' of popular religion mentioned in the previous chapter. The Owenite who sang his social hymns in the Manchester Hall of Science, was striving for much the same goals as his neighbour who sang Wesley's hymns in the Primitive Methodist chapel or listened to 'the prophet' in the Southcottians' meeting place at Ashton-under-Lyne. The injustices and enormities of early capitalist society were replaced by the dream of an earthly millennium as he sang:

Community! the joyful sound
That cheers the social band,
And spreads a holy zeal around
To dwell upon the land.

Community is labour bless'd,
Redemption from the fall;
The good of all by each possess'd,
The good of each by all.

Community is friendship's throne,
With kindred minds around:
'Tis in community alone
That friendship can abound.

Community doth wealth increase,
Extends the years of life,
Begins on earth the reign of peace,
And ends the reign of strife.

G

Community does all possess
That can to man be given;
Community is happiness,
Community is heaven.[6]

Millenarianism as a method of social change was attractive for several reasons. First, it was sudden, total and irrevocable. In this sense millennialism was a revolutionary ideology. The change envisaged was not an improvement of the present, but an utter rejection and replacement of it by something perfect. Second, this change was felt to be very near. Catastrophe was imminent, and the 'Signs of the Times' confirmed the sense of expectancy and urgency. In fact, some of the joys of heaven on earth could already be foretasted in the community or sect. Third, the change was felt to be inevitable. Objections or improbabilities were simply discountenanced, and hope was boundless, for human (sinful) nature would be transformed (or, redeemed). To the millenarian mind all issues were to be resolved in terms of absolute moral categories, a simplification which provided a powerful stimulus to action and a solution to any knotty intellectual problems which might threaten belief. The Owenite knew that he possessed the Truth, and all else was Error.

It is in this context of millenarianism that many aspects of popular expectation and striving between 1830 and 1850 have to be considered. The goals seem often to have been personal as well as social, and distinctions between individual as opposed to collective action were seldom recognised. Again, no firm line was drawn between the religious and secular spheres. The religious doctrines of conversion, salvation and the millennium could be secularised to meet the needs of communitarian socialists; the promises and threats of Chartist orators were decked out in the imagery of the Book of Revelation or the language of the Old Testament. This was not a conscious borrowing or adaptation, but a drawing upon a common culture which contained important elements of eschatology and millenarianism. Historians have noted that conditions of rapid social change encourage the formation of sects. Problems of readjustment for individuals and groups, and the fears, insecurity and general upset that accompany the interruption of normal economic and social relations probably account for the proliferation of sects at such times. The small millennial sect, withdrawn from the world and awaiting the Coming of the Kingdom, was as much part of the early Victorian scene as the huge Chartist movement, with its mass demonstrations and great public visibility. Each in its way was a response to the need for social adjustment or social change.

Some of the same qualities that made the sects attractive were also found in other social movements. The need for security and the craving for fellowship were catered for in the friendly benefit societies, which were the oldest and most numerous of the truly indigenous institutions of labouring men. In return for a small weekly or monthly contribution paid into a common fund they provided sickness and funeral benefits. The members met monthly in a local public house to transact business and, more interestingly, to drink beer and have a convivial time. An annual feast was held, and the funerals of deceased members were usually followed by a supper. Ceremony and ritual were an essential part of the societies' life. They held open air processions with bands, banners and uniforms on all possible public occasions. Indoors they conducted secret initiation rites, using mystical symbols, grandiloquent titles and regalia, mostly in imitation of the freemasons. Originally friendly societies had been local institutions with seldom more than a hundred members. But in the 1830s and 1840s these were eclipsed by the growth of the affiliated orders, with their organisation into a unity (headquarters), districts and lodges. The oldest and largest of these was the Manchester Unity, Independent Order of Oddfellows. There were also the Ancient Order of Foresters, the Loyal Order of Ancient Shepherds (Ashton Unity), the Order of Druids, the Ancient Britons, and the Antediluvian Buffaloes.

In point of numbers the friendly societies far exceeded any other social organisation except the churches. From an estimated 925,000 members in 1815 they grew to about four million in 1872 (compared with nearly 400,000 in the cooperative movement and 500,000 trade unionists in the same year). By 1842 the Manchester Unity of Oddfellows had 3,500 lodges with 220,000 members.

The strongholds of the societies were the industrial North and Midlands, and the membership was mainly from the better-off sections of the working classes. Institutionally the friendly societies were very close to trade unionism, and in some cases unions were registered as friendly societies to protect their funds. With the rise of the affiliated orders there was some friction between the lodges and the central body; and in true sectarian fashion the discontented members split off, and like the Methodists formed a new society. In general, friendly societies were not agents of social change, but rather of social adjustment. The middle classes (in contrast to their attitude towards trade unions) welcomed the friendly societies as institutions of working class self-help, while regretting that they 'wasted' time and money on conviviality. Yet without the opportunities for social intercourse which they provided, the friendly societies would not have flourished as they did. For many thousands of working men they satisfied a longing for membership of some institution to which they could feel they belonged, a place where they would be welcomed as a 'brother', not treated as a 'hand'. Such opportunities, as we have already seen, were not too numerous in the new industrial society.

The movements so far considered were predominantly working class in orientation, although Owenites eschewed any class appeal and adopted the title 'Association of All Classes of All Nations'. To complete our brief survey we need to refer to movements which originated with other groups and which had different aims and objectives. For obvious reasons the aristocracy and gentry did not need to promote social movements to advance their interests; but the middle classes, who were by no means so content with the *status quo*, had both the incentive and the means to do so. Two movements illustrate the potentialities for change via middle class efforts. The first, the Anti-Corn Law League, was an agitation to secure changes which benefited, in the first instance, the industrial middle class. The second, temperance, was pioneered by members of the lower middle classes but directed primarily at the working classes.

In many ways the Anti-Corn Law League was the middle class

counterpart of Chartism. Beginning in September 1838 as the Manchester Anti-Corn Law Association, a group of Manchester Radicals (led by J. B. Smith, George Wilson and Richard Cobden) launched a campaign to secure the repeal of the taxes on imported corn, which they regarded as pernicious and obsolescent. They argued that the Corn Laws raised the price of food, and contributed to the distress which followed the poor harvest and the onslaught of the depression in the winter of 1837–8. The Corn Laws, moreover, were designed to protect the agricultural interest at the expense of the rest of the nation, and were a blatant piece of class legislation. Free trade, so the argument ran, was the one sure way to promote industry and reduce the cost of living (and also wages, added the Chartists); the Corn Laws were a symbol of the policy of protection and aristocratic privilege. As the movement grew it became a rallying point for the whole panoply of middle class grievances. The Nonconformists were brought in with anti-state church and (Tory) parson arguments; the humanitarians and philanthropists were attracted by the case for 'scientific' as opposed to indiscriminate charity; and the advocates of international peace were assured that their cause would be best furthered by the removal of all barriers to trade and industry. The Leaguers made strenuous efforts to present their case as a national and not simply a class interest. But they failed to convince any considerable part of the working classes, who agreed rather with the Chartists that repeal should follow universal suffrage. And Manchester talk of feudal tyranny in the countryside did nothing to mollify the suspicions of the gentry that the League was an attack on the traditional control of power by the landed interest.

During its first two years the League was mainly a propagandist body. With a headquarters in Manchester and local associations in other northern and midland towns, it held meetings, employed lecturers and distributed tracts. The impact of these activities was somewhat reduced by the greater excitement aroused by Chartism, which was then at its peak. Attempts to counter Chartist influence, either through a rival body (such as the Leeds Household Suffrage Association of 1840) or by direct alliance with the Chartists (as at Birmingham in 1841–2), came to nothing; but the lesson was drawn that propaganda was not enough, and that political means would have to be employed. The political machine that the Leaguers perfected between 1842 and 1846 was a model for the conduct of a campaign to win public support and bring pressure to bear on parliament. A most efficient organisation through a central and local associations, employing full time agents and using the most up-to-date business methods went into action. Public relations were skilfully cultivated by means of lectures, publications, well-advertised conferences, and the purchase of press support. Electoral registers were closely checked to get out the free trade vote, objections raised to the claims of possible protectionist voters, and the forty shilling freehold franchise (retained, ironically, in the 1832 Reform Act as a concession to the landed interest) was exploited to create new free trade voters. The pay off came in 1846. Famine in Ireland followed the failure of the potato crop at the end of 1845, and with the urgent need for alternative cheap food, the leader of the Whigs, Lord John Russell, abandoned his opposition to further reform and supported repeal. Sir Robert Peel, the Conservative Prime Minister, had also been gradually moving towards a policy of repeal and in 1846 was able to carry such a measure through Parliament, though only at the cost of splitting his party.

The good fortune of the Leaguers in gaining their objective contrasted markedly with the failure of the Chartists to win universal suffrage. Both movements worked to apply political pressure for the remedy of economic grievances, but were also prepared to try other methods too. The League at the time of the Plug riots in 1842 toyed with the idea of encouraging a little physical force to back up their demands. John Bright, the best known Anti-Corn Law spokesman of the day, urged non-payment of taxes; and the extremist wing of the repealers urged the adoption of 'bold measures'. But the Leaguers had the great advantage over the Chartists of being the spokesmen for the dominant middle classes, backed by the power of industry, the vote and the ideology of orthodox political economy. The friends of progress and morality, like G.R.Porter and Samuel Smiles, rallied to the support of the League. As Cobden wrote in a letter to Peel, the repeal of the Corn Laws was a logical result of the passing of the Reform Bill.

The temperance movement was a middle class venture of a different kind. It arose after the passing of the Beerhouse Act of 1830, which was intended to reduce drunkenness by making it easier to buy beer rather than spirits. But the social and moral effects of drink, described in Chapter Three, were such as to convince many middle class reformers that a campaign to wean labouring men from drinking habits was an imperative duty. There was a widespread belief among practical social reformers (especially those sympathetic to Owenism) that man was often the victim of circumstances, that his conduct and beliefs were to a large extent determined by his environment, and that consequently the most effective way to eradicate anti-social attitudes and behaviour was to remove the obstacles to a happy social existence. Expenditure on drink reduced the amount of income available for other (socially preferable) activities; and excessive drinking produced social misery. Temperance was a method of tackling this social problem. For some reformers, however, the problem had another dimension: drinking was not only a social evil, it was a personal sin. The rescuing of the working classes from the demon of drink was a mission of salvation. An individualist appeal and a personal approach, culminating in signing the 'Pledge', were characteristic of this type of temperance reform. Together, the personal and social approaches constituted a powerful motivation for an anti-drink movement.

The honour of claiming the first British temperance society is usually accorded to Bradford (June 1830), but the first national body seems to have been the British and Foreign Temperance Society, which held its inaugural meeting in Exeter Hall, London, in 1831. This was an upper middle class organisation, in favour of moderation (temperance) rather than abstinence. It was soon followed by a lower middle class rival, the British Temperance Association, started by Joseph Livesey of Preston in 1835, and advocating complete abstinence (teetotal) from all alcoholic beverages. Nonconformist religious influence was strong in the

BTA, and its fanaticism offended more moderate men. Consequently a third body, the National Temperance Society, sprang up in 1842 after disputes about the use of sacramental wine. It was middle class, interdenominational, and opposed to teetotalism. Until the formation of the United Kingdom Alliance in 1853, which rapidly became the leading British temperance organisation, the movement lacked institutional unity, and its main strength, as with so many British social movements, was in the localities of the North and Midlands. The network of Bands of Hope, tract societies and Young Men's Improvement Associations built around the chapels soon became formidable auxiliaries in the battle to stamp out drink. Livesey's policy of 'moral suasion' was a combination of self-help and evangelical conversion, replete with calls to 'repent' and 'root out sin'. A vast propaganda through lectures, sermons, books, magazines and tracts was commenced. Public debates with opponents, coffee stalls, and the encouragement of leisure time activities as a counter attraction to the public house, were all grist to the temperance mill. How many people were reached by the temperance cause is impossible to determine; certainly it made an impact on the respectable, self-help sections of the working classes and on the chapel-going lower middle classes. Compared with the Anti-Corn Law League the temperance organisation of the 1840s was much less professional and stream-lined; but it was more deeply rooted, its objectives were much broader and far-reaching, and its campaign was more prolonged. Until 1853 the temperance movement as a whole did not seek legislation to outlaw or restrict the sale of drink; only later was the emphasis switched to political pressure for prohibition or a permissive bill.

Very few of the social movements of early Victorian Britain were successful in the sense that they attained their declared objectives. Only if their aims were limited to securing a particular reform or piece of legislation (the repeal of the Corn Laws, the enactment of a factory act, the abolition of the stamp duty on newspapers) did they attain any obvious victory. Movements of a perfectionist or millenarian character were by their nature precluded from such limited successes, since they aimed at nothing less than a total reconstruction of society. Nevertheless the constant striving, the restless seeking for change was in itself a significant social phenomenon, for it helped to change the prevailing sense of what was socially desirable and what was preposterous. 'What is man born for,' asked Ralph Waldo Emerson, the New England transcendentalist, 'but to be a Reformer, a Remaker of what man has made?' From America came confirmation and stimulation of the ideas of the reformers of the 1840s. The Unitarian inspiration from the writings of W. E. Channing and Theodore Parker, the American communitarian experiments of the Shakers and Fourierists, and the enthusiasm of radicals for the social seethings of Jacksonian democracy, all contributed to an ethos favourable to social reform. It is a common mistake to dismiss as fads or cranky ideas those 'isms' with which we do not sympathise, and which appear too outlandish to be taken seriously. Yet just as an extreme case of a disease is of more interest to a student of medicine than a mild dose, so minority cults and forgotten enthusiasms can remind the historian of the full implications of contemporary social trends. Who now takes seriously the pseudo-science of phrenology, which claimed to diagnose character by an examination of the bumps on the head? What of homeopathy, hydropathy ('the water cure'), mesmerism, and animal-magnetism? Vegetarianism (and Grahamism from America) went far beyond rules for a non-meat diet and provided a philosophy of health and social conduct. Ventilation and fresh air addicts explained their enthusiasms in terms of the contribution made to social progress. Sexual reform ranged from advocacy of free love in communities, to a campaign against masturbation and the elaboration of a social theory based on 'Vital Force'. Beyond the personal and idiosyncratic elements in these movements which flourished in the 1840s was a social dimension which helps us to estimate the expectations and frustrations of the men of the time.

The question, however, remains as to why the early Victorian period should have been so prolific of social movements of all kinds. Broadly the answer would seem to be that they represented a variety of responses to the experience of social and economic change of a peculiarly intense nature. It was an experience which, in various ways, set individuals and groups outside the main development of society. Their reactions were complex and can be considered from several different angles. This becomes clearer when we try to identify the particular types of people who were associated with social movements. On the one hand were supporters of movements aimed at adaptation or integration into existing society, and whose function was basically social control; these movements were commonly of an individual, personal, self-help nature. On the other hand were the members of reform movements which challenged existing authority; for them change was a liberating force, to be brought about, usually, by collective means. Members of this last group were characterised by their repudiation of traditional habits and institutions, their critical approach to contemporary society and their willingness to accept new ideas. In most modern societies these 'progressive' attitudes have been associated with three categories of people: the poor and oppressed, who struggle for economic betterment and social emancipation; sensitive members of the more affluent classes whose consciences are aroused by the poverty, misery and injustice they see around them; and the intellectuals whose critical faculties are excited by the mediocrity, inefficiency and self-deception of the defenders of the *status quo*. Early Victorian reform movements contained all three elements, though not in equal proportions nor always in convenient class categories. The depressed handworkers and unemployed factory operatives who formed the mass following of Northern Chartism obviously belonged to the first category; Lord Shaftesbury and the Evangelical factory reformers to the second; and John Stuart Mill and the Benthamite utilitarians to the third.

Yet if our analysis stopped at this point a vital aspect of the dynamics of reform movements in the 1830s and 1840s would be missed. Time and again the historian is impressed by the frequency with which the same men turn up as the leaders, especially at the local level, of successive reform movements. It is also clear that a majority of them belonged to that group of the 'middling classes', composed of better-off artisans, small tradesmen and shopmen, who formed the backbone of most radical causes. They were independent, often individualistic, and non-deferential. They valued respectability and practised self-help. A few of them, mostly shopkeepers, had the vote (under the £10 householder qualification of the 1832 Reform Act) but for the most part they were disfranchised unless they could qualify as freemen of some ancient borough. They were literate, self-educated, and addicted to philosophic radicalism (utilitarianism) in its popular forms. In religious belief they were nonconformist or agnostic. Typical figures were Henry Hetherington, Francis Place, William Lovett, Thomas Cooper, Joseph Barker and J.A.Roebuck, but the list could be vastly extended. Corresponding to this thumbnail biographical pattern was a radical recipe used many times over as a programme in different movements: extension of the franchise, cheap and efficient government, disestablishment of the Church of England and religious freedom, education for all, temperance, and free trade – all of which would promote prosperity, happiness and international peace. The central core of artisan/lower middle class reformers was joined by other 'natural' radicals from proletarian and affluent middle class backgrounds. As they exhausted the possibilities of one movement they moved on to the next, searching for a solution that usually seemed to elude them, yet confident of ultimate success.

This last observation suggests that reform movements had a function other than the purely instrumental, that they satisfied certain needs irrespective of whether or not they attained their stated objectives.[7] Involvement in a particular movement implied more than support for a set of specific demands. It was a token of a man's position on a whole range of issues, a sign of his dissent from the dominant values associated with the central institutions of society, such as monarchy, aristocracy, private property, capitalism, religion. Transfer from one movement to another did not signify a change of heart, but rather a new assessment of the best means towards a constant overall goal. To men like Ben Wilson of Halifax, the Chartist movement did not appear as a failure. Looking back from the vantage point of the 1880s, he recalled:

> The Chartists were called ugly names, the swinish multitude, unwashed and levellers. . . . What they wanted was a voice in making the laws they were called upon to obey; they believed that taxation without representation was tyranny, and ought to be resisted; they took a leading part in agitating in favour of the ten hours question, the repeal of the taxes on knowledge, education, cooperation, civil and religious liberty and the land question, for they were the true pioneers in all the great movements of their time.[8]

Chartism, together with other reform bodies, social movements and the nonconformist chapels, provided a range of satisfactions. They acclimatised their members to democratic practices and procedures; they offered fellowship and the opportunity to find self-achievement; they brought a little dignity and colour into what was otherwise a rather drab existence. These were benefits irrespective of the actual goals of the movement, and in addition to any specific material gains that might be won. Many of the movements of the 1830s and 1840s were noticeably very loosely organised. They had followers and supporters rather than members, and their characteristic activities were large meetings and public demonstrations. For many of the middle class activists the satisfactions were of a psychological nature: the sense of involvement, the happiness in struggle, and the moral compulsion to battle for righteousness. The dissenting tradition (political, social and religious) was firmly rooted in Britain by 1830. It had been built by people who were in some way outside of, or estranged from certain central aspects of British life, and who maintained a critical attitude and were prepared to crusade against what they considered injustices. The early Victorian reformers added a new and glorious chapter to this ancient tradition.

To close on this note, however, would be a serious distortion of the record. For there were, as always, far more people who uncritically endorsed the institutions and values of the *status quo* than reformers. Despite the strong impetus to reform after 1830, the strength and particularly the resilience of the basic institutions of British life were sufficient to weather the storm. Stability, law and order were maintained, though only just. The process of conflict and adjustment between classes and groups had been very acute, probably more so than at any other time in British history. Ultimately a *modus vivendi* was worked out, and the gentry, middle classes, artisans and labouring poor learned to live with one another. But in 1848 (the Year of Revolutions) it had seemed a near thing. Compared with other industrial societies (America, Germany, Russia) Britain appears to be remarkably homogeneous; but the early Victorians were conscious mainly of their divisions and conflicts. Only occasionally, as when they paused to survey themselves at the Great Exhibition, did a few of them glimpse the social perspective of their unique position as the richest and most privileged nation in the wealthiest area of the world. From the majority such glimpses were hidden. They would have agreed rather with the immigrant girl in Australia in 1846: 'I know what England is. Old England is a fine place for the rich, but the Lord help the poor.'[9]

Notes

1 The Social Experience of Industrialism

1 The most convenient source for the population statistics used in this chapter is B. R. Mitchell and Phyllis Deane, *Abstract of British Historical Statistics* (Cambridge, 1962).

2 *Rural Rides* (London, 1830), 31 August, 1 September 1826.

3 T. R. Malthus, *An Essay on the Principle of Population* (4th ed., London, 1807), p. 19.

4 William Thomas Thornton, *Over-Population and its Remedy* (London, 1846), p. 268.

5 W. W. Rostow, *Stages of Economic Growth* (Cambridge, 1960).

6 E.g. W. W. Rostow, *British Economy of the Nineteenth Century* (Oxford, 1961), pp. 123–5.

7 E. P. Thompson, *The Making of the English Working Class* (London, 1963), p. 12.

8 For a perceptive analysis of the problems of industrialism and urbanisation, to which I am indebted, see Eric E. Lampard, 'The Social Impact of Industrial Revolution', in Melvin Kranzberg and Carroll W. Pursell (eds.), *Technology in Western Civilization* (Madison, Wis., 1967); and 'American Historians and the Study of Urbanization', in *The American Historical Review*, vol. LXVII, no. 1 (October, 1961).

9 Friedrich Engels, *The Condition of the Working Class in England* (1845), trans. and ed. W. O. Henderson and W. H. Chaloner (Oxford, 1958), p. 30.

10 R. Whately Cooke-Taylor, *Introduction to a History of the Factory System* (London, 1886), p. 31.

11 W. Cooke Taylor, *Notes of a Tour in the Manufacturing Districts of Lancashire* (London, 1842), pp. 4, 5, 7.

12 William Dodd, *The Factory System Illustrated* (London, 1842), pp. 2, 80–1.

13 James Kay Shuttleworth, 1832, as quoted in Asa Briggs, *The Age of Improvement* (London, 1959), p. 61.

2 Patterns of Poverty

1 Arthur Young, *A Tour through the East of England* (London, 1771), vol. IV, p. 361, and quoted in S. & B. Webb, *English Poor Law History*, Part I.

2 Henry Mayhew, *London Labour and the London Poor* (London, 1862), Extra vol., p. 10.

3 *Ibid.*, vol. III, p. 243.

4 Cooke Taylor, *Notes of a Tour*, pp. 30–6.

5 Dodd, *The Factory System Illustrated*, pp. 108–10.

6 *Report . . . by a Statistical Committee of the Leeds Town Council*, in, *Journal of the Statistical Society of London*, II (1839–40).

7 P. Horsman, *Machinery: Its Effects upon Society*. MS. lecture, Yorkshire Union of Mechanics' Institutes.

8 Engels, *The Condition of the Working Class in England*, p. 157.

9 Thomas Cooper, *Life, Written by Himself* (London, 1872), pp. 140–2.

10 James Caird, *English Agriculture in 1850–51* (London, 1851), p. 287.

11 *Ibid.*, p. 310.

12 *Ploughing and Sowing. By a Clergyman's Daughter* (London and Derby, 1861), p. 1.

13 William Howitt, *The Rural Life of England* (2 vols, London, 1838), I, 157–8.

14 In this account I have drawn heavily on the excellent monograph by Terry Coleman, *The Railway Navvies* (London, 1965).

15 Mayhew, *London Labour and the London Poor*, III, 257.

16 *Ibid.*, III, 263–4.

17 C. Turner Thackrah, *The Effects of the Principal Arts, Trades and Professions . . . on Health and Longevity* (London, 1831), p. 119.

18 Mayhew, *London Labour and the London Poor*, III, 379.

3 The Condition-of-England Question

1 Thomas Carlyle, *Chartism* (London, 1839), p. 3.

2 G. K. Chesterton, 'The Secret People', *Poems* (London, 1915).

3 *Annual Report of the Domestic Mission Society* (Leeds, 1858), p. 13.
4 *Report . . . by a Statistical Committee of the Leeds Town Council*, p. 402.
5 *Report on the Condition of the Residences of the Labouring Classes in the Town of Leeds* (London, 1842), p. 18.
6 *Leeds Intelligencer*, 15 February 1851.
7 Chadwick, *Report on the Sanitary Condition of the Labouring Population of Great Britain* (London, 1842), p. 160.
8 Rev. M. C. F. Morris, *The British Workman Past and Present* (London, 1928), p. 3.
9 S. R. Bosanquet, *The Rights of the Poor and Christian Almsgiving Vindicated* (London, 1841), p. 91, quoted in John Burnett, *Plenty and Want* (London, 1966, reprinted 1968), p. 68, to which I am indebted for material on dietary changes and food adulteration.
10 Mayhew, *London Labour and the London Poor*, III, 250.
11 *Ibid.*, p. 420.
12 John Dunlop, *Philosophy of Artificial and Compulsory Drinking Usage in Great Britain and Ireland* (London, 6th ed., 1839), p. 3.
13 P. Gaskell, *Manufacturing Population of England* (London, 1833), p. 7.
14 *Ibid.*, p. 19.
15 See Neil J. Smelser, *Social Change in the Industrial Revolution* (London, 1959), chapters 9–11.
16 *Hansard*, 1844, vol. LXXIII, col. 1092, quoted in Margaret Hewitt, *Wives and Mothers in Victorian Industry* (London, 1959), p. 31.
17 Gaskell, *Manufacturing Population*, p. 57.
18 Mayhew, I, 40.
19 Carlyle, *Chartism*, p. 12.
20 *Ibid.*, p. 16.

4 *Patterns of Prosperity*

1 Howitt, *Rural Life of England*, II, 126–9
2 The following analysis of landed society has drawn heavily on F. M. L. Thompson's *English Landed Society in the Nineteenth Century* (London and Toronto, 1963), to which I am much indebted.
3 Howitt, *Rural Life*, I, 22.
4 Anna Maria Fay, *Victorian Days in England: Letters of an American Girl, 1851–52* (Boston and New York, 1923), p. 16.

5 *Ibid,,* pp. 49–50
6 Sir John E. Eardley Wilmot, Bart, *Reminiscences of the Late Thomas Assheton Smith, Esq.* (London, 3rd ed., 1862), p. 18.
7 *Ibid.*, p. 123.
8 See the excellent study by J. A. Banks, *Prosperity and Parenthood* (London, 1954) upon which I have drawn in the second half of this chapter.
9 Anthony Trollope, *An Autobiography* (Edinburgh and London, 1883), chapter VII.
10 Charles Dickens, *The Posthumous Papers of the Pickwick Club* (London, 1836–7, New Oxford Illustrated Dickens, 1948), chapter 58.
11 Alexis Soyer, *The Modern Housewife, or Ménagère* (London, 1849. 'Thirty second thousand', 1856), pp. 413–15.
12 E. P. Thompson, *The Making of the English Working Class* (London, 1963), pp. 9–11.
13 Mayhew brothers, *The Greatest Plague in Life* (London, 1847), pp. 24–5.
14 Charles Kingsley; *His Letters and Mèmories of His Life*, ed. by His Wife [Fanny Kingsley], (2 vols, London, 1877), I, pp. 190, 255.
15 R. H. Tawney, *The Acquisitive Society* (London, 1921), p. 3.
16 C. Woodham Smith, *Florence Nightingale* (London, 1950), p. 93.
17 Quoted in Royal Commission on Population, *Report*, Cmnd. 7695 (London, 1949), p. 38.
18 See p. 4.
19 Sir Edward Cook, *The Life of Florence Nightingale* (2 vols, London, 1913), p. 103.
20 Trollope, *Autobiography*, p. 49.
21 William Acton, *Prostitution, considered in its Moral, Social, and Sanitary Aspects* (London, 1857), pp. 72, 73.

5 Early Victorian Values

1 *Census of Religious Worship. England and Wales. Report and Tables* (London, 1853).
2 Arthur Miall, *Life of Edward Miall* (London, 1884), p. 151.
3 A. P. Stanley, *Life of Thomas Arnold* (London, 1904 edition), p. 278.
4 W. R. W. Stephens, *The Life and Letters of Walter Farquhar Hook* (London, one vol. edition, 1885), p. 241.

5 For biographical details see J. T. Barker (ed.), *Life of Joseph Barker, Written by Himself* (London, 1880).

6 Benjamin Wilson, *The Struggles of an Old Chartist* (Halifax, 1887), p. 3.

7 William Lovett, *Life and Struggles* (London, 1876), p. 37.

8 Timothy Claxton, *Hints to Mechanics on Self Education and Mutual Instruction* (London, 1844), p. 7.

9 Joseph Lawson, *Progress in Pudsey during the Last Sixty Years* (Stanningley, 1887), p. 39.

10 *Howitt's Journal*, I (1847), Weekly Record, 17 April 1847, p. 32.

11 Samuel Smiles, *Self-Help* (London, 1859), p. 46.

12 Quoted in Yvonne Ffrench, *The Great Exhibition: 1851* (London, 1950), p. 190.

6 Social Change and Social Movements

1 In this discussion of social mobility I have been greatly helped by the work of Stephan Thernstrom on similar movements in America. See Stephan Thernstrom, *Progress and Poverty* (Cambridge, Mass., 1964).

2 *Transactions of the National Association for the Promotion of Social Science* (London, 1859), pp. 340–5.

3 *The People*, II (1850), pp. 378–9.

4 W. E. Adams, *Memoirs of a Social Atom* (2 vols, London, 1903), I, p. 237.

5 R. G. Gammage, *History of the Chartist Movement* (Newcastle, 1894), p. 94.

6 *Social Hymns: for the use of the Friends of the Rational System of Society* (Leeds, 2nd ed., 1840), no. 129.

7 For a stimulating discussion of this theme, see Frank Parkin, *Middle Class Radicalism* (Manchester, 1968). The book is a study of the Campaign for Nuclear Disarmament.

8 Wilson, *The Struggles of an Old Chartist*, p. 14.

9 Margaret Kiddle, *Caroline Chisholm* (Melbourne, Australia, 1950), p. 243.

Suggestions for Further Reading

1. General works covering the period

Briggs, Asa. *The Age of Improvement* (London, 1959).
Checkland, S. G. *The Rise of Industrial Society in England, 1815–1885* (London, 1964).
Dodds, J. W. *The Age of Paradox: a Biography of England, 1841–1851* (London, 1953).
Woodward, E. L. *The Age of Reform, 1815–1870* (Oxford, 1938).
Young, G. M. *Victorian England: Portrait of an Age* (London, 1936, 2nd ed., 1953).
(ed.) *Early Victorian England, 1830–1865* (2 vols, London, 1934).

2. Books on particular topics

Beales, H. L. *The Early English Socialists* (London, 1933).
Briggs, Asa. *Victorian Cities* (London, 1963).
(ed.) *Chartist Studies* (London, 1959).
Burnett, John. *Plenty and Want: a Social History of Diet in England from 1815 to the Present Day* (London, 1966, reprinted 1968).
Chadwick, William Owen. *The Victorian Church*, Part I (London, 1966).
Chambers, J. D. *The Workshop of the World* (London, 1961).
Clapham, J. H. *An Economic History of Modern Britain.* Vol. I. *The Early Railway Age, 1820–50* (Cambridge, 1926).
Cole, G. D. H. *A Short History of the British Working Class Movement* (London, 1948).
Coleman, Terry. *The Railway Navvies* (London, 1965).
Court, W. H. B. *A Concise Economic History of Britain from 1750 to Recent Times* (Cambridge, 1954).
Driver, Cecil H. *Tory Radical: the Life of Richard Oastler* (New York, 1946).

Edwards, Maldwyn. *After Wesley* (London, 1948).

Ffrench, Yvonne. *The Great Exhibition: 1851* (London, 1950).

Glass, D. V. (ed.) *Introduction to Malthus* (London, 1953).

Gloag, John E. *Victorian Comfort* (London, 1961).
   Victorian Taste (London, 1962).

Hammond, J. L. and B. *The Age of the Chartists, 1832–1854* (London, 1930).

Harrison, J. F. C. *Robert Owen and the Owenites in Britain and America* (London, 1969).

Hewitt, Margaret. *Wives and Mothers in Victorian Industry* (London, 1959).

Hobhouse, Christopher. *1851 and the Crystal Palace* (London, 1950).

Hobsbawm, E. J. *Labouring Men* (London, 1964).
   Industry and Empire (London, 1968).

Hovell, Mark. *The Chartist Movement* (Manchester, 2nd ed., 1925).

McCord, Norman. *The Anti-Corn Law League, 1838–1846* (London, 1958).

Marcus, Steven. *The Other Victorians* (London, 1966).

Schoyen, A. R. *The Chartist Challenge: a Portrait of George Julian Harney* (London, 1958).

Smelser, Neil J. *Social Change in the Industrial Revolution* (London, 1959).

Thompson, E. P. *The Making of the English Working Class* (London, 1963).

Thompson, F. M. L. *English Landed Society in the Nineteenth Century* (London, 1963).

Ward, J. T. *The Factory Movement, 1830–1855* (London, 1962).

Wearmouth, R. F. *Methodism and the Working-Class Movements of England, 1800–1850* (London, 1937).

3. Some contemporary works.

Carlyle, Thomas, *Chartism* (1839); *Past and Present* (1843) [various modern editions].

Chadwick, Edwin. *Report on the Sanitary condition of the Labouring Population of Great Britain* (1842), ed. M. W. Flinn (Edinburgh, 1965).

Dickens, Charles. *Dombey and Son* (1848) [many later editions].
   Oliver Twist (1837–8).

Disraeli, Benjamin. *Sybil; or the Two Nations* (1845) [reprinted in Worlds Classics and other editions].

Engels, Friedrich. *The Condition of the Working Class in England* (1845), trans. and ed. W. O. Henderson and W. H. Chaloner (Oxford, 1958).

Gaskell, Elizabeth Cleghorn. *North and South* (1855) [numerous later reprints].

Lovett, William. *Life and Struggles* (1876), ed. R. H. Tawney (2 vols, London, 1920).

Mayhew, Henry. *London Labour and the London Poor* (3 vols and extra vol., London, 1861–2, 1864) [Reprinted 1969. Also selections edited by Peter Quennell as *London's Underworld* (London, 1952), *Mayhew's Characters* (London, 1955), and *Mayhew's London* (London, 1949).]

Surtees, R. S. *Handley Cross* (1843) [steadily reprinted in the nineteenth century and today].

Index

Wales, xvii, 2, 36, 96
Wage slavery, 70
Wars, Napoleonic, 29, 80, 161
Weather, effect of, 49
Wealth, alliance of new and old, 96–9
Wellington, Duke of, xvi, 96, 152
Wesley, John, 127, 165
Westminster Review, 120, 133
Whigs, 13, 97, 152, 158
Whitworth, Joseph, 11
Wilson, Benjamin, 160; *Struggles*, 130, 175–6
Wiltshire, 38
Women, workers, 26–8, 42, 45–6, 73–7; middle class, 115–19; single, 116–18
Woodhead tunnel, 40
Woolcombers, 25, 38
Worcester, Marquis of, 91
Work, gospel of, 140–42
Work discipline, 129, 135

Workhouses, 51–2, 81–5; Andover, 84; Hoo Union, 84
Working classes, xviii, 19–86; assimilation to industrial society, 135–6; movements of, 153–68; poets, 139; standard of living, 55–6; and Methodism, 128–30; self-help, 142–4; social mobility, 148–9
Wroeites, 131

York, 37, 61, 102–3, 130
York and North Midland Railway, 102
Yorkshire, 5, 16, 28, 30, 36; East Riding, 37–8, 63–4, 128; North Riding, 37–8; West Riding, 16, 29–30, 36–8, 42, 64, 126–30, 138–9, 155–6
Young, Arthur, 20
Young, G. M., xv
Y.M.C.A., *Lectures to Young Men*, 140